How to Get a Better Job

How to Get a Better Job

by AUSTIN MARSHALL

THE NEW OFFICIAL BOOK
of
THE JOB SERVICES CENTER
formerly THE JOB FINDING FORUM
of
THE ADVERTISING CLUB OF NEW YORK

HAWTHORN BOOKS, INC.
Publishers / NEW YORK

Library of Congress Catalog Card Number: 64-13794

ISBN: 0-8015-3774-6

3 4 5 6 7 8 9 10

To

M. A. M.

Foreword

The Advertising Club of New York points with special pride to the Job Services Center, formerly the Job Finding Forum, which has been one of the most productive public service programs in our long history.

For nearly forty years, this service has helped thousands of men and women to help themselves and each other to more rewarding, challenging positions in every conceivable kind of professional work in industry and nonprofit endeavors.

We appreciate the commendations of many distinguished leaders representing different fields of American enterprise and service:

Nelson Rockefeller has referred to the club service as "an impressive help in the establishment of a dynamic labor market to meet the growing needs of our nation."

Dr. William Menninger described it as a highly constructive effort with a phenomenal record of helping men and women who want to better themselves."

We are grateful for the help and encouragement of nationally recognized personalities. But our service is not conducted by leaders or teachers or professionals. It is made up of people like you and me working together to ferret out the problems of career planning and job finding.

Our meetings are guided by moderators and panels composed mostly of appreciative, successful job seekers who found their way to better positions using our proven methods. In the weekly sessions one individual at a time presents his or her experience. A discussion centers around the particular circumstances; achievement records are reviewed; job campaigns are discussed; résumés and letters are criticized; and sometimes there's a mock interview if the job hunter is one who seems to have difficulty communicating with prospective employers.

Some of our people have advanced a step or more in their already established fields—sometimes with the same employer. Secretaries have moved up to administrative assistants; assistant managers have attained managerial status; executives have become vice presidents.

Others have changed fields to venture into different work: teachers have become sales personnel; government people have converted their experiences to commercial jobs; housewives have applied their "home work" to salaried positions; a minister changed to fund raising.

Still others have converted their avocational interests to paying jobs: camera bugs have become photojournalists; self-styled writers have found editorial positions; a hi-fi fan sold his knowledge as an audio technician to a convention hall; a dedicated bird watcher went to work for the Audubon Society.

Other job-finding groups sponsored by civic and business organizations, trade and professional associations, and some college alumni chapters have been organized and patterned after our format. The service has reached across the country from New York to San Francisco, where the Junior Chamber of Commerce sponsors one of the most successful Job Finding Forums.

Of course, we're more organized now than we were in the beginning. The sessions are too big to run them casually. Our earlier trial and error methods have been honed to professional techniques, and through the years many job-finding experts have generously contributed their time to help us establish the best possible service.

The author of this book, Austin Marshall, himself a Forum graduate and an honored member of the Advertising Club of New York, has continued widespread, intensive research on the subject. The old Job Finding Forum has a new name, Job Services Center, with many additional features and updated methods included in this new revised edition of *How To Get A Better Job*.

Mr. Marshall is a popular speaker on Career Planning and Job Finding. His articles and features have appeared in many trade and professional magazines and have been syndicated in Sunday newspaper supplements.

Now he has organized the best of his practical experience and writings in these chapters for your reading and reference at home.

Make this book your companion. And when you get your new job, lend a hand to the next fellow.

MICHAEL A. CHAMBERLAIN,
President, Advertising Club of New York

Preface

The techniques in this book have been developed through the years by many dedicated Forum workers assisted by a number of distinguished professional personnel specialists who have generously contributed their knowledge.

The Job Finding Forum was organized as a Community service by the Advertising Club of New York. It has spanned the country where other Forums have been patterned on the same format and sponsored by various civic and business organizations, trade and professional associations, and some colleges.

If you are interested in organizing a Job Finding Forum, write to:

The Chairman
The Job Services Center
Advertising Club of New York
23 Park Avenue
New York, New York 10016

The Chairman
The Job Services Center
Junior Chamber of Commerce
333 Pine Street
San Francisco, Calif. 94104

Acknowledgments

I want to than all of the volunteer Job Finding Forum and Job Services Center workers, past and present—the moderators, panelists, lecturers, committee members, and the many regular meeting participants who have given so much of their time and service. This is, indeed, their book as well as mine.

We all owe a debt of gratitude to the founder of the Job Finding Forum, John H. Ryder, for his years of leadership and inspiring belief in the principles of give and take which are still the keys to the Job Services Center. Special appreciation is further expressed to Dr. Niki Kominik, Alex Jones, securities broker with Dean, Witter & Co., Margaret MacKinnon, director of employee relations, Lord & Taylor, and Leon Theil, public relations executive and vice president, Manning, Selvage & Lee, Inc., for their dedicated and outstanding work as chairpeople. And I certainly acknowledge the particular services of Norbert Delville, international marketing consultant, Robert Reuss, assistant vice president, (retired), Bankers Trust Co., Dr. Charles Proudfit and Lois Arndt, United States Information Service.

It has also been a privilege to exchange ideas and methods with colleagues affiliated with the Man Marketing Clinic sponsored by the Sales Executive Club, the Forty-Plus Club, the former Career Planning Clinic sponsored by the Notre Dame Alumni, and with Charles Clark, management education specialist with B. F. Goodrich Company.

Through the years I have gained very helpful insights from many long interviews with professional advisers—employment agents, recruiting specialists, management consultants, vocational guidance counselors, job evaluation experts, psychologists, and company personnel executives. They are too numerous to mention individually but all of them have generously contributed their knowedgeable points of view. I especially acknowledge Dr. Paul Proctor, personnel psychologist, and Mr. Robert Sheehan, senior principal librarian, New York Public Library.

Some distinguished people gave me help and encouragement from the beginning. They are Dr. W. Kenneth Riland, United States Steel Corporation and authors Catherine Marshall, Lavinia Dobler and Margaret Kreig.

For additional advice and assistance in preparing this revised edition, I extend my thanks particularly to Robert J. Ely, director of international, Railroad Products Group, Abex Corporation and to Jeanne Hammond, whose experience and achievements among women in the working world updated my perspective considerably.

Lastly, I am grateful to the successful job finders who contributed their résumés and letters as samples that add importantly to this book as a practical guide.

Contents

How to Get a Better Job

CHAPTER I

How Do You Compare With Other Job Hunters?

Just starting?
Stalled in mid-career?
Faced with a personal problem?
You are not unique. Others have been there before.

A sudden turn of events may have forced you to find a job for the first time in years. And you really don't know much about this business of job finding. Or perhaps job finding has been a frequently recurring challenge for you. And on more than one occasion, you've discovered yourself thumbing through the Help Wanted ads, following up leads, and taking the stand before a jury of interviewers.

You may be a young job hunter hesitating at the starting line. You may be stalled in mid-career. Or you may be an old-timer halted in your path by the rush of younger candidates. Whatever your particular situation, take a hard objective look and you will probably discover that there is nothing at all unique about it.

Of all the men and women who have come to our Job Finding Forums through nearly a quarter of a century, the individual with the unusual problem is the exception. For every newcomer, there was someone just before him and there will be someone just after him in the same personal predicament, almost down to the last detail.

Thousands of our Forum people, only partially discontented with their jobs, have found more interesting work at better pay, with greater freedom from company politics and office personality clashes. Many others, trapped in total job dissatisfaction, have actually altered the course of their lives.

One man, at the peak of frustration on a job, left the office without notice, swept up his wife and children, and went for a nineteen-day Caribbean cruise. When he got back, the cupboard was bare, but with a new perspective and the step-by-step procedure which is outlined in this book, he plotted his way to a more rewarding position than he'd ever held before.

A young man who had flunked out of a large company training program came to our Forum and graduated with a new job in an entirely different line of work.

A widow with three dependent children found a good job— her first in eleven years.

One bachelor, twenty years in what he described as "standing still and bored in just a job," started a new career for himself.

"But," you retort, "you don't know what my problem is. I happen to be caught in a practically unheard of predicament." While this could be true, it's highly unlikely.

If you are a beginner, you're surrounded by young people with the same questions and doubts that are holding you back. Many of these persons have resolved their confusion by using the methods in this book.

If you are fairly well along in your career but not quite able to get over that next higher hurdle, you are not alone. Practically every week, others in the same situation manage to find a good new job with the planning and follow up described in these pages.

If you've held a variety of jobs, there are plenty of white collar workers who weave a oneness out of such a mixture. If your intended career got side tracked, there are lots of men and women who either retrace their steps or adapt their special talents and interests to a more satisfying job.

If you are under pressure and working excessive overtime, there are many others who find ways to convert too-hard-earned success into more enjoyable work.

If you've committed an indiscretion at the office which you

think all employers will hold against you, just remember that everybody has a skeleton in the closet. And employers aren't looking for skeletons.

If you have a domestic, financial, or personal health problem, make a little survey of your successful friends. You'll be surprised to find out how many of them were once in the same spot.

Nearly everybody has been challenged to make a consequential job change at one time or another. Some are compelled by their own conscience or practical needs to move on to more rewarding positions. Others are forced by circumstances beyond their control. Whether you get fired or resign isn't usually regarded as much more than a technicality. Whether the landlord dispossesses you or you move voluntarily, the process of throwing away worn-out things and packing up the more useful items is the same.

And this is exactly how successful job finders in our Forums have planned their way out of a situation like yours and into the right job.

Welcome to the fraternity. Start your new job campaign with the suggestions in the next chapter.

CHAPTER II

What it Takes to Get a Better Job

How much work?
How much time?
How are you fixed for cash?

NO matter what you have heard or seen advertised, there is no such thing as a package of instant magic which will wrap up the perfect job for you overnight. If you're really serious about finding the place where your particular talents and interests can be applied and where you'll get the rewards you rightfully deserve, be prepared for some work.

It's true that some people marry the boss's daughter or slip into a family business or pick up a lucky phone number and win a job. Some people win at horse races too. But if you want to control your career rather than gamble on it, finding a good job calls for planning and organizing a step by step program.

This begins with an important soul search and self-appraisal. Then it involves a methodical job research to select the right prospects. There are résumés and letters, sometimes job-finding portfolios, and even Situation Wanted ads, to be prepared in a way which will direct attention to the best you have to offer. And, of course, there is interviewing to be done, an art in itself. In fact, there are a hundred and one tricks in executing each of these steps to sell yourself for all you're worth.

The whole procedure need not be a long drawn-out process, but it can take time. And if you want to avoid excessive anxieties at the end, set yourself a reasonable time limit at the beginning.

6

Read through this book quickly first and estimate how much time each step will take you.

Generally speaking, the length of time it takes to get a good new job will depend on the amount of your experience and your salary requirements and the extent of the change you decide to make in your work.

When you have little or no experience, job opportunities may seem to appear frequently. But it is essential to determine whether or not these openings are indeed opportunities. Unless you feel pretty certain of a particular job, it's advisable to take a month or so, to weigh various possibilities. Don't allow yourself to be persuaded immediately. And don't worry about losing out because you hesitate or remain undecided. You may lose one job this way, but at your level there will be others.

When you've had considerable experience, job finding takes longer. Employers don't hand out the larger pieces of pie as readily as they do the smaller ones. At this level, your prospects may deliberate over your qualifications at greater length and be slower to come to a final decision. Remember this, if you must wait longer for their verdict than you had expected.

If you're planning to advance in pretty much the same general line of work, the length of time your search will take may depend largely on how quick you are to grasp the perspective of the higher level position. It's a much bigger step from second lieutenant to first lieutenant than most job hunters realize. Higher level jobs not only call for additional responsibility but, more significantly, usually involve a different kind of activity, sometimes entirely different. Years of experience alone don't qualify you for that job. You have to understand and think in terms of a new assignment. And you have to demonstrate that your talents, interests and experience qualify you for another kind of job, not just a bigger one.

There's a natural tendency on the part of most job applicants to review the past rather than concentrating on the future. The task at hand calls for attention to the next job, sizing up your prospect's needs and understanding what you will be called on to do for him. Always keep this in mind in your job-finding campaign, and you'll save yourself a great deal of time.

The same thing applies to any consequential job switch. If you're moving from non-profit work to a commercial field, you have to sound commercial. If your experience has been overseas and you want a better job in this country, you have to translate your qualifications into domestic language. If you're changing from your own business or free-lance work to a payroll job, you have to think and sound like an organization man. To imagine yourself on the next job and to visualize what you would be doing there, are the quickest ways to make it a reality.

We'd like to remind you that the amount of time you allot for job finding and career improvement must be determined in part by a realistic appraisal of your personal finances. We are continually surprised at the number of Forum newcomers who have given very little consideration to budgeting themselves through a job-finding campaign. If you try to conduct a job campaign without including some semblance of a financial plan, you're likely to subject yourself to added pressures at a time when it is a decided advantage to weigh matters cautiously and thoroughly.

When you plan a vacation, you estimate what it will cost first. When you decide that you need a bigger home or a better apartment, you determine the price range first. And when you want a better job, some sort of a financial program is necessary to sustain yourself and your dependents through a specified period.

"That's all very well," you say, "but *I'm* flat broke! I got fired unexpectedly a long while back and I've used up all my reserves."

Be honest with yourself. How severe *is* your state of financial emergency? Are you sure that you can't stretch things farther or possibly dig up a little extra if it is absolutely necessary? Figure it out realistically. Start with that irreducible minimum which you must have to get by on. Exactly what is that figure for the next two weeks? What is it for a month? Maybe your first figures don't look too encouraging. If so, go over them again. This is a pretty critical time for you.

The surest way to sell yourself short is to grab the first job you can get. This can also lead back to your original predicament.

Cut every corner. Use every possible means—part-time work, a temporary assignment, unemployment insurance, even a small loan from a friend. Anything to give you time to search out the more satisfying and rewarding job. Your whole future may be at stake right now. Invest all that you can in it. Don't run, *walk* carefully to your next job.

If you have a job and a little money set aside and question whether or not it's advisable to quit so that you can concentrate full time on finding a new job, the answer is "no." While the adage that "It's easier to get a job when you have one" is not necessarily true, by holding your present position at least for a while, you can avoid money worries while you're working out those first all-important decisions and starting on some research.

If the things which are bothering you about the present job are so disturbing that you can't seem to concentrate on anything else, you may have legitimate reason to leave. But make sure you are leaving for a new job, rather than just getting away from where you are now. Some people have an advance idea of when they will leave their present job, either by notice from the employer or by their own decision. This seems to work out quite well, allowing them spare time in the beginning to carry out the ground work and then, later on, permitting them full time to sprint to the finish.

Whatever your financial condition may be, estimate your job-finding budget to last to the end of your campaign. In the beginning, job finding can be like an exciting new hobby. The exercise of spelling out your past accomplishments in an Achievement Record and résumé can be pleasantly reassuring. Those first responses from your letters and phone calls are most encouraging. It looks like a cinch. You think you've got it made. And perhaps you have.

But as in all campaigns, the last mile can sometimes get a little rough. Time goes by. One employer you expected to interview next Tuesday is called out of town for a week. Another becomes involved in business matters so that he is forced to delay considering your application a few more days. A dependent relative becomes sick and starts piling up a big medical bill.

Most job hunters run into these annoyances toward the end of the campaign. Don't be overconcerned if they happen to you. Prepare for them by working out a rough time schedule and financial plan in advance.

CHAPTER III

What Do You *Want* to Do?

How to appraise yourself with an Achievement Record.
How to execute a radical career change.

UNLESS you have a clear concept of the job direction you want to take, it's a good idea to start your campaign with some honest soul searching for what it is you really like to do and can do well. The success of every job campaign hinges on these basic issues. Writing out an achievement record will help you either verify your present decision or, perhaps, establish a new direction altogether.

Get out some paper and make four columns with the headings shown on page 12.

Notice that your achievement record is going to include not only pay jobs but possibly some hobbies or volunteer work in which you have shown consequential accomplishment and skill.

As you begin to fill in the blanks, do not attempt a chronological order. Instead, list the activities in the order of their meaningfulness to you. The first activity you mention could be something you accomplished five or ten years ago. Go back into your past as far as you like. Describe at least four activities and preferably more. Skip any job you want to forget unless some part of the work was particularly enjoyable and represents one of your important capabilities. In such a case, just mention that one phase of the work, not the whole job.

While you're reviewing your experience, you might make a note of some of those little accomplishments you like to talk about in conversation. It doesn't matter how small they may be

Job Hobby Volunteer Work	What I Did	Results And Recognition	What Features of the Work I Enjoyed Most

so long as you can show measurable achievement in the "Results" column. And it doesn't make any difference for the moment whether you think these things have any bearing at all on your career or next job.

As remote as it may seem, if you once climbed a difficult mountain and reached the peak in unusually good time, you may have put something behind that effort which can be applied to earning a living. That "something" is the type of thing you're searching for in your achievement record. Brag all you want. Nobody but you is going to see this. Just make sure you can substantiate your boast with proof. There are lots of people who brag about their automobile driving ability but their record of fender dents, prematurely worn out tires and brakes, and traffic violations doesn't project good driving at all as others see it.

In the first column, title the activity briefly in any language you will understand when you read it back to yourself. In the second column, use short phrases or words to list what you did. Sometimes it's easiest to decribe it step-by-step so you don't overlook part of it. For example, if amateur photography is one of the activities, this work might be described, "photographed, developed negatives, printed, enlarged, etc."

Under "Results and Recognition," measure the scope of this activity in terms of the amount of time spent or volume of work produced. Then specify anything you can think of to prove you did a good job. No matter what kind of work is involved, if you feel you did a good job, you probably have good reasons for it. If it was a pay job, "Results And Recognition" might include promotions, raises, commendations, time saved, money earned or saved for the employer, new business acquired, repeat customers, increased business or any other factual detail which illustrates your success.

If it was a hobby or some sort of volunteer work, "Results and Recognition" might include citations, prizes, awards, commendations, election to office or appointment to committees, re-election, reappointment, as well as published articles about your accomplishment. But by "commendation" we don't necessarily mean a testimonial dinner. It could simply be a remark which someone of recognizable authority made in passing. And don't forget to indicate the over-all time which was involved or the volume of work which was produced. The more "Results and Recognition" you can show the better, so long as you are truthful.

In the last column, "What Features of the Work I Most Enjoyed", don't try to make order out of it or attempt to be analytical about it at this point. Write your notes in key words for your own reference. When listing your likes, you might want to mention something as broad and general as "working with people" or as specific as "answering telephone inquiries." Write whatever comes to your mind without dwelling on it.

After you have at least one page of notes, though preferably more, check first over the "Results and Recognition" column to decide whether in each case your proof statements are sufficiently strong to represent a level commensurate with your occupational ambitions. For instance, if you're looking for a good job somewhere in mid-career, that mountain you may have mentioned must be a sizeable mountain, not just a mole hill; and your accomplishment in having reached the peak must be something more than an ordinary mountain climb. If it isn't, and you can't make something more of it in your proof statements, cross it off your list and go on to the next activity.

Next, and most importantly, study that last "What I Enjoyed" category. Get out another piece of paper and write a refinement of this column. Be more precise now. For instance, if you simply indicated in one place that you enjoyed "working with people," narrow the circumstances down. Did you mean that you liked to work with groups or with individuals? And what kind of people are you talking about? Do you like to seek out these people or do you prefer to have them come to you? Do you like to teach or do you like to interview? Do you like to sell to them or do you prefer to buy from them? What exactly do you mean by "working with people?"

If you mentioned something as general as having enjoyed the challenge or the response you got from the work, exactly what challenge and what response are you talking about? Question yourself and define specifically everything you have mentioned in this column.

When you've finished, review the whole column to look for common denominators. Check what it is you've enjoyed the most and oftenest in each activity you mentioned. It may take a little while to get the pattern in focus, but it's very likely to be there and well worth your concentrating to find it.

This pattern is your guide post. Your next job should include at least some of the major likes which you've listed. If it does not, you're probably headed in the wrong direction.

Perhaps you've saved some visual mementos ranging from conference programs to congratulatory telegrams. Or maybe you have stored away some kind of printed matter you've worked on, an office bulletin board notice, a company news letter, a published article, or a whole book. Open your old trunk, take these things out of hiding, and review them along with the common denominators in what you liked and did well in your work and hobbies.

A designer-artist at our Forum told us about an assortment of items she had worked on through the years and saved for "no special reason" she could think of. "I sort of liked them and guess I was proud of those particular ones," she remarked vaguely.

After preparing an achievement record, she took out this collection of objects and placed them on the living room floor to illustrate what she had written in the "What I Enjoyed" column. There were some doll dresses she had fashioned for adult appeal and which had been written up in a women's magazine. There were some greeting cards she'd made and marketed quite successfully some years before. There were a few gift packages she had designed which were used on a television show recently.

There was a little silver ring and semi-precious stone jewelry she had designed and made in college.

"Why have I hung on to these particular things?" she asked herself. "What do they have in common?"

At first, it seemed impossible to visualize any single pattern or common denominator in these very different items. But she left the objects sprawled out on the floor. She examined them a few minutes each morning over coffee and again at night when she came home. Then the picture clarified itself. These things did have something in common. Each was important to the designer because of color, texture, and the fact that they were all three-dimensional objects she'd made with her hands.

These elements were the clues. They matched the last column in her achievement record and were behind her decision for a new career. She is now a highly successful package designer for a leading cosmetic manufacturer. Before, she had been pushing along only fairly well and not happily as an assistant art director for a magazine.

While you may not be an artist or designer, it will probably pay you well to work out and examine your achievement record with the same patience and thoughtful objectivity. We've known job applicants to struggle with résumés, letters, and interviews for months without getting anywhere simply because they didn't *like* the work they were applying for. They didn't really want to do it. And no matter how much experience you have had, it's difficult to be convincing and sell yourself into a good new job if you don't honestly want to do the work you're talking about to your prospects.

Start your own achievement record now. Before you do so, however, look over this one which helped a salesman select a new career for himself.

This achievement record continued two and a half pages in the same manner. And most of the listed activities repeated the same obvious pattern emphasizing a predominating interest in the creative aspects of the work, especially that part having to

Job Hobby Volunteer Work	What I Did	Results and Recognition	What Features of the Work I Enjoyed Most
Selling local newspaper advertising	Sought new leads, made cold calls, worked out my own sales presentations, worked with layout artists, wrote some headlines and copy, suggested type.	5 years, 4 promotions and salary increases, worked from bottom to top man on a 12 man staff, brought in about 10 consequential new advertisers.	Making sales presentations, working with layout artists, selecting type, writing copy and headlines.
Photography	Photographed, developed and printed candid shots at special affairs, weddings of friends, etc. Made up and bound albums of photographs, montages, etc.	Off and on for 10 years in spare time. When friends saw my first albums, 3 others asked for them. After the first two years, I sold my services professionally, averaged 4 weddings a year in my spare time. Sometimes duplicate and triplicate orders of albums were requested.	The finish work, printing, cropping and enlarging. Making up the albums.
Selling Yellow Phone Book advertising space	Sold by phone and in person calls, suggested headlines and copy. Worked with layout artists, suggested type.	5 years, increased space about 30% above what it was when I started. Was promoted and assigned bigger territory my third year. Brought in about 60 new large and small advertisers in 2 years. Actual space increase about one fourth above the previous record for that territory.	Working out the headlines and copy and working with artists on layouts. Selecting type.

17

do with visuals. This applicant was a Yellow Pages phone book salesman with a mediocre job when he first came to our Forum. Though he thought of himself as a salesman, he was more than plainly a salesman—for he was decidedly more interested in the creating than in the selling.

He had been aware of his enthusiasm for creating visuals. But he thought of this as a personal side line quite apart from his pay job. It took the exercise of preparing and studying an achievement record to bring out the things which actually interested him. And with his new perspective, he began the search for a new position where the decided emphasis was on creating visuals.

Now, eleven years later, he is vice president of a firm which creates and produces elaborate brochures to illustrate annual stock holder statements for large companies. His principal work is supervising the creative visual production. His secondary function is selling his firm's services. The horse and cart are in proper order, and his small firm has more customers than they can handle. Among his clients are some well known national corporations, a far cry indeed from the Yellow Pages of a local phone book.

Perhaps there is some phase of your background, some consistent pattern of likes and capabilities which you should examine more closely with the possibility of putting them in the right order to get a better job.

We aren't suggesting that you sit back with pencil and paper and dream up some glorified new job based only upon your achievement record findings. Of course, you have to match your interests and likes with the realistic job market.

But your dream job may not be as far away as you think. Many of our Forum people have plotted a course to a new career through a series of interim or bridge jobs leading eventually to their desired goal. This is a stepping stone procedure to get you some experience in the new direction and, at the same time, avoid an excessive loss of income on the way.

One, not so young, reasonably successful radio station disc jockey came to our Forum complaining he was tired of his job which consisted of "talking about nothing."

He didn't like the pay, the hours, the atmosphere, the people, or anything else about the job. All he knew was he wanted "out."

When he got the gripes off his chest he was able to look *forward* to the places he might go. With the help of a long achievement record, he decided he wanted to be a person-to-person salesman, and he further concluded that he'd like to sell building materials.

This seemed far removed from being a disc jockey, but he had been a do-it-yourself remodeler around his home for a long time and especially enjoyed working with construction materials. Interestingly enough, the bulk of his achievement record centered around this hobby rather than his job. We persuaded him that the best way to make the radical job switch was by taking one step at a time and utilizing some one area of his previous experience in each step. This is the way to maintain, or nearly maintain, one's income level when making advancements into a new field. It is something like walking in a very slow wedding procession. Put one foot out ahead, and hold the other foot firmly on the ground so that you won't lose your balance before you are ready for the next step.

Our disc jockey's first bridge job was selling music library supplies and equipment to radio stations. He got this job through his knowledge of the stations and their library needs—in other words, an established "market knowledge."

After he acquired some selling experience, he got himself a second bridge job, selling unassembled plywood and Formica cabinets, tables, and record files to radio stations for their libraries and studios. You will notice that this job was a step closer to building materials. But he still hung fast to his strongest qualification—the "market knowledge" of radio stations.

Here, he established a record not only as a salesman but as a salesman of building materials. And then he was in a position to drop the last traces of his original field, the radio stations. He was prepared for the big step, his new market. And he at last became an industrial sales representative for a manufacturer of building materials after three jobs and three and a half years.

His first step, as is sometimes the case, imposed a small income sacrifice, but that was for less than a year, and by the second step he was back at his old income level in a new and what he called very exciting job. The last we heard, he was eastern sales manager for a large plywood manufacturer.

Many others like him have done the same thing, starting with the revelations of an achievement record and job research and progressing through a process of bridge jobs. You probably can work out your own decisions and plans to earn a more rewarding career this way. Give it a try by yourself first. If you encounter extreme difficulty in making the right decisions and in matching your likes with actual job availabilities, you may be justified in turning to one of the professional helps.

CHAPTER IV

What You Should Know About the Professionals

What about those psychological tests?
Do you need a guidance counselor?
Should you use a professional résumé writer?
Can you rely on employment agents and other personnel
recruiters for advice?

IF, *after* you have tried your best, you suspect there is some
area where you need professional consultation, be sure to get
the right help for your particular needs. Then, return to this
book, and carry your job-finding campaign the rest of the way
by yourself.

Before you seek any kind of professional help, there are two
things you must consider.

First, it is urgent for you to have every confidence in the
service you employ. You must be sold on your counselors. Before
you get involved with them, you must feel receptive to the advice
they're going to provide. It won't do you any good to pay money
for counsel and then decide later that because you don't like what
they told you you're going to try some other way. Obvious as
this would seem, there are hundreds of job hunters who do precisely this and wind up with nothing more than an extra bill to
pay at a time when it's hardest to pay it.

Second, there is no bona fide service which will enable you to
sit in a chair while somebody else makes your decisions, does your
work, and hands you a wonderful new job. The legitimate services
act as coaches. They will try to show you *how*, and offer some
encouragement. But none of them can play the game for you.

Some men and women who have been dissatisfied with professional help have found their way to our Job Services Center. Their principal difficulty most often turns out to be not the fault of the professional guidance they received before they joined us, but rather that they wanted to have a job found for them.

There are all kinds of professional assistants to help you in one phase or another of your job-finding campaign. There are Psychological Testing & Advising Institutes, Career Guidance Counselors, Executive Development Consultants, Personnel Search Specialists, Job-Prospect Mailing-List Houses, State and Federal Employment Services, Commercial Employment Agencies, and more.

Some are entirely legitimate. Their methods have been checked and have stood the test of time. Their advice is reliable. Others are highly questionable. Their procedures are founded on individual opinions and pet theories. Their counsel can do you more harm than good. Which is which? Exactly what service do they perform? How much does it cost?

1. *The Vocational Testing and Advising Services*

Suppose you find yourself in some unusual difficulty in determining what your topmost capabilities actually are and what kind of work really suits you best; and let us assume this is a logical point in your life at which to pause for an objective view of yourself. One good device for this purpose is aptitude and vocational interest testing, followed by professional advice based on the results of the tests.

There are several types of highly respected institutes and centers offering this kind of service. On top of the list of reputable testing centers are those sponsored by colleges and universities. And similar excellent service organizations are operated by private commercial consultants, as well as by non-profit civic and religious-affiliated organizations.

To find any one of these testing services, simply look under

"Vocational Guidance & Career Guidance" in the yellow pages of the telephone directory for the largest city near you or call the college or university in your area.

Whichever source of information you use, the most reliable key to reputable services is accreditation by the *American Personnel & Guidance Association*. When you find one or another testing center which looks good to you, ask if they are so accredited. If you have any difficulty determining this, go to the reference room of the nearest large library. Ask for the *Directory of Counseling Services* published by the International Association of Counseling Services and check that organization. If your library does not have this directory, you can get a copy by writing the American Personnel & Guidance Association, 1607 New Hampshire Ave., Northwest, Washington, D.C. 20009. The charge for the directory is $4.00.

Recognition by the APGA is not necessarily the final criterion for judging every testing and advising service, especially some of the very small consultant organizations and individual practitioners. Some of these smaller services are perfectly legitimate and competent. Unfortunately, however, there is no reference for you to determine the good ones and you have to resort to individual opinions to find them. If you are considering non-accredited organizations or individual practitioners, check on them very carefully and use more than one source. A faker in this field can be dangerous.

Generally speaking, most of the accredited and well-established testing and advising centers offer similar programs designed to fit your individual needs. When you inquire of an organization, ask exactly what their program consists of. A standard one will be something like this:

ADVANCE PREPARATION

You complete a detailed biographical questionnaire, usually at home.

PRELIMINARY INTERVIEW

You participate in a private conference of approximately one hour to draw out more information about your background, to select the tests best suited to your particular circumstances and to understand the context in which the test findings are to be evaluated and discussed later on.

TESTING

You take a series of written and oral tests concerned with your individual abilities, interests, and personality. The average program includes twelve to fifteen hours of tests which can be taken in two or three days but which are better spread out over several days to avoid fatigue in any one session.

POST TESTING CONFERENCE

After the tests have been scored, you participate in a summary conference of one to two hours with a thoroughly trained counselor. This session is for the purpose of interpreting and discussing the test results, making general recommendations with respect to your career and, sometimes, making general recommendations regarding a feasible plan for you to follow.

Most testing and advising centers will arrange for later additional conferences if you feel you need them to confirm your direction and procedure. Understand, however, that this type of service does not include any job prospect contacting, or job-finding, or specific employment help for you.

SUMMARY REPORT IN WRITING

For your review and future reference, some centers will provide a written report summarizing the test findings, the discussion, and the recommendations based on them.

There you have an outline of what to expect in a well-planned testing and advising program. There are some variants in this format from one testing center to another, but any program which is much short of the above is probably not the best you can get.

The total cost of this complete program varies with the sponsoring organization. Subsidized nonprofit centers such as those conducted by the Federation Employment & Guidance Service and B'nai B'rith Career & Counseling Services range from seventy-five dollars upward, based on your income. Other nonprofit centers such as those sponsored by colleges and universities cost generally one hundred twenty-five dollars, while private commercial institutes charge approximately two hundred to four hundred dollars depending on how much counseling follows the tests. In fact, with the exception of the strictly nonprofit clinics, there is an extra charge for additional follow-up conferences *after* the one post-testing conference described above.

The difference in charges from one testing center to the next is not necessarily an indication of the quality or completeness of the service. The less expensive centers often have waiting lists and their procedures can involve delays of several days between steps. The more expensive institutes are more likely available to serve you on short notice and can complete your program much faster.

As a word of caution, it is not feasible to carry out this kind of program by mail. While a correspondence course might seem convenient, you run the risk of more damage than constructive help. It is well worth traveling fifty or a hundred miles for this kind of assistance, if you feel you want it.

Before you decide on a testing and advising program, there are some observations you should consider. Some tests and testing procedures are very well established and have proven their validity beyond question, and the experts are continually making progress with new developments in areas of vital concern to job hunter and employer alike. But even the testers are not entirely in agreement as to what test is best for what purpose, and there remains a difference of opinion regarding interpretation and follow-up counsel. This is one good reason for you to choose an APGA accredited testing organization where procedures are uniform and based on the most reliable standards.

Employers across the country are also in disagreement with respect to tests and testers generally. Some highly successful and reputable employers will not hire any important white collar worker until the applicant has been subjected to a battery of tests and recommended for the job as a result. These employers, especially the ones who hire a large number of employees, claim that the test procedure improves the odds in recruiting the right people for the right job. Just as many reputable employers feel that the tests are not satisfactorily applicable to their recruiting needs and they don't use them at all.

This difference of opinion among the people who are doing the hiring might in itself give you reason to question the benefits of the tests when it comes to making your own decision about taking them. But the tests and testers are here to stay, and you might be one who can gain from them.

We feel that the tests help most but not all of the people who take them. Some job hunters come out with a clearer sense of direction and more confidence in what their next job target should be. There's nothing more valuable to carry into a job interview than a real conviction as to what you want to do. Other job hunters seem to get little from testing and counseling. In some instances, their failure to get constructive help may be due to a misunderstanding as to how the service works.

It is essential to realize that usually the tests and those who interpret them do not dictate a final answer or a one, two, three formula for you to follow. They only form a more dependable basis upon which you can make your career decisions more objectively than you can by guessing about yourself.

Some people complain that the tests didn't reveal anything which they didn't already know about themselves. It's true that the test findings may coincide with your own self appraisal. In fact, if they don't, there is either something wrong with the tests or with what you've been thinking about yourself. However, scientific tests can add significant details to your own appraisal. They can spell out your capabilities and interests more precisely than you can yourself, and they can bring into focus highlights which you haven't recognized.

Still other job hunters have told us they didn't think the test findings and interpretations were correct. But this again may be a failure to understand and use the service properly. If you have a disagreement with the tests or take exception to some of the conference comments, by all means go back and talk with your counselor. One or two repeat conferences may clarify these doubtful points for you and the counselor.

A lot of us get caught in circumstances that cloud the basic issues which must be decided first in any job-finding campaign. If after you've tried hard on your own, worked out an achievement record, and talked things over with friends and family, you still feel confused about what kind of work is best for you, by all means avail yourself of a bona fide testing and counseling service.

Select a reliable service. Make a date for a preliminary interview. They will tell you honestly whether or not they think their service will be helpful to you. You have no commitment beyond this first interview.

2. Commercial Career Advancement Services

You may find yourself well along in a career which you suspect is not going in quite the right direction. Or perhaps you feel you're in the right direction but not making the headway you should. Or maybe after a number of years in one kind of work, you are obliged to re-adapt your experience to a very different kind of employment. Indeed, maybe you've tried several times to make a major adjustment. Perhaps you've changed jobs and still don't seem to come out where you belong.

Is something dragging? You know perfectly well the potential is there. But the results aren't.

After you've tried on your own for what seems like too long a time in too short a life and you still feel you need help concerning the whole job problem from beginning to end, you might consider the executive development consultants.

If you do:

You should have a potential salary of not much less than $20,000 annually.

You should feel wholeheartedly receptive to their methods and counsel.

You must be able to afford their fees.

To find the reputable consultants in this category, look for their advertisements in the "Business" or "Classified" sections of the large Sunday newspapers. In many cases, you will find that the advertising of the more dependable and well-established executive development consultants is distinguished by the following points: The better services often use larger advertising space. The copy stresses "executive development" and "career adjustment" rather than "résumés or "job-prospect lists." Some good ones refer to recognition they have received from business and professional associations or from well-known publications.

You will also notice that some advertisements offer a free booklet. Send for it and see what it says. Investigate further. Find out how long the service has been in business. The most substantial ones have a record of at least ten or fifteen years. Determine the qualifications of their counselors. Do they have advance training at recognized academic institutions?

Check the consultant you have in mind with organizations like The American Management Association, The American Society of Training Directors, and The Society for Advancement of Management. One of these associations will probably have an office in the large city near you.

Don't give up if the first reference you check doesn't provide a satisfactory answer. Organizations like the three listed above are sometimes hesitant to endorse any executive development consultant. But they know the good ones and will tell you what you want to find out if you prod them politely.

Finally, look into the step-by-step service offered by the consultant you are considering. The most complete service includes a program something like this:

First, a preliminary interview of a half hour or more. This conference is to determine what you need and whether or not they can provide it. It is for you to find out how much it will cost and how long it will take. Like other reliable service organizations in this career planning and adjustment field, dependable executive development consultants will tell you honestly whether or not they feel you can benefit from their particular service.

The best programs offered by these organizations begin by giving you a detailed biographical questionnaire to fill out at home and exercises designed to assist you in listing your achievements objectively and factually.

This early work is usually followed by one or more hour-long sessions of private consultation devoted primarily to helping you to define your interests and to describe your capabilities effectively. Then, the course moves into the area of determining who can use what you have to offer. What field? What organization in that field? What job in that organization?

As the procedure continues, you receive counsel in lining up the right prospects and in preparing the tools you need to demonstrate your qualifications. You are also advised on how to sell yourself in interviews. Finally, in some instances, you receive additional counsel after you're on the new job and getting adjusted to it.

The cost of this service is fairly uniform from one consultant to the next. And it's high.

An introductory consultation is often free of charge. An average minimum course of about nine months and including approximately a dozen hour-long conferences with an unlimited number of brief consultations ranges from $500 to $1000. For an average maximum course of about a year with possibly 30 hour-long conferences and an unlimited number of brief consultations the cost will be about $2000 or more.

The variations in cost depend on the extent of the counseling and how much of a job change you decide to make. It is a long and thorough process, but if you are not working at the time you start, some of the best consultants will help you find a temporary position. Understand, however, that these counselors are not employment agents and do not act in this capacity.

Many of the steps in these courses are like those set forth by the Job Finding Forum. The advantage of using an executive development consultant is the personal attention you get. The outstanding consultant firms in this field employ well-grounded systems and proven techniques. Their staff counselors are trained to draw out the best in you. Their fingers are on the pulse of business, science, and the professional fields. And, a good deal of their time is devoted to study and research in various occupational categories. Your course with them is planned with very realistic goals for you.

The disadvantage in resorting to help of this kind is that you may become dependent on other people to resolve your career difficulties. Experienced consultants know this perfectly well and they try to make *you* do the work. Inadvertently, however, as time goes by, they often wind up forcing your hand when you get stuck. Obviously, your career isn't going to be a success if you turn back to a "pro" every time you have difficulty.

There are times when all of us can benefit from a little personal attention and tutoring in areas where we don't happen to be particularly proficient. And this is just what the good executive development conselors can offer you. They concentrate on strengthening your weak spots. And sometimes, for good reason, job hunters are not receptive to the well-meaning advice of friends, family, and business associates. When it comes to resolving a career problem, some people quite logically prefer objective, professional counseling. If you feel this will be helpful to you, you will find that most of these executive consultants will arrange a free preliminary interview.

3. *Vocational Guidance Counselors*

In addition to the first two professional services we have just discussed, there is a wide variety of so-called vocational guidance counselors.

There are too many classifications of these to list them individually here. Some are very small consultant firms. Others operate as private practitioners. Their qualifications range from training in applied psychology to research in job markets. A number claim possession of special job prospect mailing lists and other ins.

Whatever their specialty or however capable and well established they may be, it doesn't seem advisable for you to place your career future in the hands of one self-styled expert or a very small organization. We remind you again that it takes a careful mixture of components to make a job-finding campaign successful. It's hard to get this much symphony out of a one-man band. For this reason, the most reputable private practitioners will stick to their one specialty and advise you to go elsewhere to work out other phases of your job-finding project.

As a fair warning, this field attracts a good number of quacks, operating under the too often abused heading of applied psychologists. Some make all sorts of remarkable, positive warranties regarding their techniques and methods, but remember that nobody in this field can perform miracles.

While you can spot the wild-claim prestidigitator merely by the feeling that he is exaggerating, there are other borderline operators not so easy to recognize. These are the self-made counselors who claim practical experience and sometimes boast a little formal training in counseling. But they are not qualified by their own personal orientation to advise others.

When we refer to counselors unqualified by "their own personal orientation," we mean the men and women whose own lives are not sufficiently resolved for them to be able to offer objective advice without, consciously or subconsciously, inflicting their own disturbances upon the people they advise.

It takes a great deal of personal resolve and self-discipline to make a good counselor. Many so-called counselors go into this field to compensate for their own inadequacies by telling other people what to do. They are like so many of our acquaintances who seem compelled to give us unsolicited advice. You are far better off to sweat out your own decisions than to rely on a counselor like this.

As a final word of caution, if you do find a good counselor, make certain you understand what the charges will be. The best way to determine fair price for services offered is to do some comparative shopping with the previously mentioned organizations—what precisely are the charges, exactly what service or services are included, step-by-step and over how long a period of time.

4. Catalyst-National Network of Local Resource Centers

For women, Catalyst is an excellent national network of Vocational Guidance Centers. It is a nonprofit organization that helps expand career opportunities for college-educated women. The centers are either free or charge very minimal fees. Many of them are sponsored by colleges and universities. To locate the center nearest you, write Catalyst National Headquarters, 14 East 60th St., New York, New York 10022. Ask for the list of their local area addresses.

5. Professional Résumé Writers

Here's where we draw the line between what is constructive help and what isn't because:

Nobody can prepare a better résumé for you than you with an honest effort can prepare for yourself.

The practice you get in working out your own good résumé will improve your ability to speak for yourself from that first phone call to the last interview.

Perhaps as a last resort, after you have organized the substance of your résumé yourself, you can use just a little help with the finished writing. But don't be lazy about this either. Spell it out in your own language if you want to distinguish yourself from the mob.

A long while back in our Job Finding Forum work, we discovered the futility of hiring a résumé writer. And we are reminded of it over and over again whenever a job hunter shows up with a professionally prepared résumé.

John Neville, a research chemist, came to us after many months of job scouting without success. John read his résumé aloud to our group for criticism and suggestions. When he finished reading, the room was silent. It was one of the best résumés we had reviewed in some time. No one could find any fault with it or add anything helpful.

Indeed, it was a good résumé. In fact, it had been getting John Neville into interview after interview—and with the right people, too. But John never came out of any of the interviews with a job.

As we talked with him about his job hunting experiences, it gradually became evident that John didn't sound like his résumé. The résumé was precise. John was vague. The résumé was interesting. John was bored. The résumé looked neat as it should have, but John needed a shave and a haircut. The résumé was perfectly honest and factual, but it just wasn't "John"—because John wasn't the author. Little wonder, then, that the résumé got the interviews but *John* never got the job.

After that, John Neville started from scratch and made his own decisions, carried out his own job research, and wrote his own résumé. He began to sell himself. The résumé he prepared for himself was no slick professional document. It wasn't even a good amateur presentation. But it was John himself, and at his best. A short while after he finished it, he got the job he wanted.

Ten years later, John Neville returned to pay us a visit. He was with the same company and had advanced successfully. We asked him what he thought had been the most helpful single thing he had gained from our methods and techniques. He replied with a sheepish grin, "Well, for one thing, I learned to write my own stuff and I've been doing it ever since."

You will do a lot better if you learn to write your own material now, and you'll save yourself some money as well. There is one rare exception. If, suddenly and unexpectedly, you are requested by some employer to furnish a résumé immediately for a specific job opening, you may be justified in hiring a "pro." If so, be very careful whom you select. If you know a personnel expert or an employment recruiter whom you can trust, ask him to recommend a résumé writer. Or, you can find numerous "résumé services" advertised in the phone book yellow pages and in the business section of your Sunday newspaper. Some of these advertisers are legitimate résumé printers and reproducers. They do not "write" résumés. They only reproduce them. And that's *all* they advertise. Call a few of them. Without identifying yourself, tell them what you're after. Ask them who they recommend. They may furnish the names of a few résumé writers.

But, beware that some of these people advertise "résumé reproduction" as a front for all kinds of side deals they'll try to sell you. Their advertising is for the sole purpose of getting you to visit them in person. Some will tell you they "happen to have" an excellent list of prospective employers—for a price. Others will pose as personnel recruiting representatives for a whole segment of employers in your field. They will offer to promote you with these employers—for an advance fee. This procedure, incidentally, is illegal in most states. Still others will advertise themselves as expert résumé writers who promise remarkable results.

Use your own good judgment. Skip the ones who exaggerate. Check the charges of any résumé writing service you are considering. Some operators will try to take you for as much as two hundred dollars to write your résumé, especially if they have reason to suspect that you have money and are in a hurry.

Actually, there is no set fee for résumé writing. Some of the pros will update an old résumé for twenty-five dollars. In fairness to the legitimate practitioners, their fee must depend on your particular background. If your career has progressed in a clearly defined pattern in one field and without too many job

changes, an experienced résumé writer can compose an acceptable chronological résumé for you in a few hours. If your background is more complicated with a number of job changes and
in quite different kinds of work, it will take a longer time and
demand a larger fee. Up to $300 is justified if it takes repeated
hour-long interviews with you to compose an attention-getting
résumé.

In any case, no résumé writer can quote you a price until he
knows your background. For this purpose, you'll have to name
employers and specify dates. Just be careful with whom you
speak and you'll be all right.

5. Employment Agents and Personnel Recruiters

There are more than a dozen kinds of professional services
whose business is filling specific job openings. Among these are
commercial employment agents, company recruiters, and management consultants who specialize in a personnel search for their
clients. Also on the list are the state employment services, and
the placement bureaus run by professional and trade organizations, schools and colleges.

Most of these services function primarily, or solely, as media
to establish contact between employer and job hunter. And you
might very possibly want to use some of them to locate available
jobs—*after* you have determined what it is you *want* to do and
can do well.

But, for now, understand that it is not a good idea to depend
on the advice of these people in making your fundamental career
decisions. It is not wise to let them influence you with respect
to the kind of work you ought to be doing. Even when it comes
to a specific job opening, it isn't good practice to accept a
recruiter's recommendations without carefully weighing what the
job actually *is* against what you have previously decided is the
right job for you.

Independent commercial employment agents, as well as company recruiters and management consultants who work for the
employer, have more concern for the employer than for you. And,

what's good for the employer isn't necessarily what's best for
you. To stay in business, the independent agent must satisfy the
employer first because the employer is the agent's regular customer. You are only transient business. A recruiter who works
for the employer earns his living by serving that employer's interests. It is, understandably, his job to sell you on accepting a position with an organization for that organization's welfare, not
necessarily for your own. Any good agent or recruiter will consider your wants and be honest with respect to the potential a
particular job has for you. But remember that no matter how
conscientious the recruiter may be, if he's going to earn his living
he's got to satisfy the employer first.

Too, the competent recruiting agents know their job markets,
job specifications, and job evaluations—and they know how to
size up job applicants. But they do not know *you!*

No matter how experienced they may be, it is not possible
for one of them to learn much of consequence about your subtle
needs in the short time allotted for an interview. Even if they
could spend more time with you in interviews, these people are
not qualified to make judgment or offer counsel with respect to
your personal necessities and wants.

So make your career decisions before you talk with agents and
recruiters. The "pros" can be very persuasive when they put a
tempting job in front of you despite the fact that it is not the
kind of job you have planned for at all. Take aim in advance and
stick to your guns.

In looking back over the professional career-planning and job-
finding services we have discussed, you notice we have emphasized and re-emphasized that you alone must be responsible for
your own decisions. You, yourself, must do most of the work it
takes to get the job you want. When you go into that final interview, you do not go in there with a favorable test report tucked
under your arm, a sympathetic guidance counselor holding your

hand, and an eager employment agent shoving you from behind. You go alone!

If you have leaned too heavily on the advice of a guidance counselor, your interview presentation will sound like the counselor, instead of like you. And if you parrot the words of some employment agent, this may be obvious to the interviewer without your realizing it. So be yourself! Do as much as you possibly can on your own. Go into your job interview with your own well-thought-out convictions. And be prepared to speak for yourself if you want to come out from that interview with the job.

CHAPTER V

The Importance of Research

For the young job hunter.
For those in mid-career.
And for the old-timer.

DON'T make the mistake of scratching around on the surface when you're looking for valuable contacts and good job prospects. Of course it may be helpful to ask among your friends and scan the employment listings and possibly talk to some agents and recruiters. But this kind of scattered inquiry will not penetrate the surface very far. Moreover, it can actually be misleading.

You are not very likely to stumble into a good job by mentioning your availability to a few friends here and there. It isn't probable that the right prospects will drop into your lap from a Position Wanted ad which you casually toss into some publication. And you can't very well control your career future by running your finger down a list of Help Wanted ads and stopping where something strikes your fancy.

You are making a carefully calculated estimate of who can use your services and why. Such an estimate calls for planned, organized research. Thousands of job hunters waste a tremendous amount of time and energy chasing in vain after jobs which have been created out of imagination—jobs which in reality either don't exist at all or only partly exist so that the applicant's qualifications don't quite fit the job. Some get interviews and are almost hired several times. Others manage to get a job only to discover later after the honeymoon is over that they made a wrong guess or "something was misunderstood."

Above all, be aware that many job hunters sell themselves short because they think they know their field pretty well and are in too much of a hurry to explore further. Find out more than you know now about your chosen field, more than you know now about individual organizations in that field, more than you know now about the people who run those organizations.

From the outset of your job hunt, take the time to compose as complete and as accurate a picture as you can of this kind of information. It is much like a jigsaw puzzle. You may have nothing more than what looks like a hopeless mess of fragments to begin with. Once you get the first few pieces locked together it can be quite interesting. Just don't try to squeeze one of those little pieces into a place where it doesn't quite belong. Take the time to find the right pieces and to insert them correctly.

If you pursue your job research faithfully, we can promise you that you'll save hours and days, possibly even months, of writing résumés, and getting interviews. You will also show yourself to far better advantage once you get into the interviews.

If you are a young job hunter feeling your way in the working world, your best bet by far is to look beneath the surface. We aren't suggesting that you can come up with all the answers for your future, but those first job moves are important and it's a pretty good idea to watch where you are stepping very carefully. Don't lean too heavily on the counsel of a mere handful of well-meaning advisers. Get a broader consensus. Get more facts. Find out for yourself. If perhaps it's a training program which you are considering, don't accept it at face value. Is it really a training program or is it only a pool for mailroom attendants?

If you have reached the half-way mark in your career and you want a better job, this is the time for you to climb a little higher for a broader view. Examine more of the trade professional publications than you ordinarily read. Ask more questions of yourself and of others. Make some more new personal contacts even if you already know a lot of the right people in the field.

Naturally, you have certain already-established financial obligations. And, in the final analysis, the job which you decide upon will have to meet at least your minimum monetary requirements. But, if you're really serious about getting on a new employer's better payroll, do not start your job research centering it around a predetermined dollar sign. When you permit a specified salary to be your first concern you may be sidestepping the more important issue of what it is you honestly like to do and want to do. So, begin your investigation with a free hand. Let yourself go, without any brakes on at the start, without any self-imposed financial barriers. Then, as you progress, you'll be surprised to find how the money problem takes care of itself.

If you are an old-timer with many years of experience, it is essential for you to bring your perspective up-to-date now by double-checking to make sure that you do indeed know your field and can realistically estimate your rightful, logical place in it. This is especially true if you have been associated with one organization for a long time. Be aware that other employers probably do things quite differently from the way you are used to doing them, sometimes in pretty subtle ways. Their policies are different. Their routine procedures are different. Their organizational framework is different. Make it your first concern now to search out those differences so that you are equipped to show how your know-how is applicable to them.

You do indeed have substantial experience which no young man can offer. The way to make it of value to a new employer is to demonstrate how that background can be put to profitable use for him now. Research will bring out his problems and his way of doing things so that you can talk with him about his immediate needs instead of talking at him about your life history.

We would not deny that being over age is one of the many standard job finding problems. But, despite what you may have heard to the contrary, if you can convince an employer that he can use your experience profitably, he, in turn, can by-pass company pension systems and other so-called age rules and policies. It's being done every day.

Whatever your situation may be, whether you're a young beginner or an old veteran of many job wars, start this job campaign with research. Except for rare, isolated instances stick to research until you can name usually not less than six prospects and the reasons why and how each of them might be likely to use your services.

If you have a knack for detective work and digging out facts and clues, use it for all it's worth, which is plenty. If research doesn't come naturally to you, discipline yourself and learn how. Begin by following the suggestions in the next chapter. Then use your imagination. And you'll be surprised how adept you can become in a matter of two or three days.

CHAPTER VI

How to Research Your Next Job

The four information channels: friends and acquaintances; trade and professional associations; the newsstand; and libraries—what you can learn from these.

Begin your research with a general investigation as if you weren't looking for a job but rather just trying to improve your knowledge. Don't be in a rush to pin-point one particular job immediately.

If you're quite certain of your next job direction, verify your decision by turning now to the questions starting on page 43 in this chapter. Can you answer these questions?

However, if you're undecided about your career or thinking about a marked change, you'll do well first to scan one or two of the better published lists of "careers and jobs" to get a realistic picture of the possibilities. One good list is *You and Your Career* by Professor H. Alan Robinson of Hofstra College, published by *Collier's Encyclopedia.* Look it over at the library. Another useful list is *The Occupational Outook Handbook,* published by the Bureau of Labor Statistics in Washington. Thumb through this volume at the library. Or write to the Superintendent of Documents, U.S. Government Printing Office, Public Documents Department, Washington, D.C. 20402 if you wish to purchase individual listings of occupations which interest you. The price per listing is twenty-five to thirty cents.

There are books about various fields written by leaders in the fields. Glance through one or two if you wish. But no more than lightly, as they are too general for your purpose. Dozens of undecided job hunters have arrived at our Forums for the first time with volumes of this sort. One week they appear with a "fascinating" book on *The Romance of Banking,* the next week with two books, one written by "the world's most successful salesman" and another called *Landscape Gardening for Profit.* Around and around they go as if they were trying to postpone a decision and avoid what has to be done to *get a job.*

If you find yourself circling around in excessive book reading instead of job hunting, it might be helpful to seek out one of the legitimate counselors.

The way to get a realistic concept of fields and careers is to find out more about the *jobs* in them. This is also one of the best ways to resolve what you want to do. The more information you get now, the better prepared you'll be when you meet in interview with your prospects. Whether you are a beginner or a veteran with years of experience your success in those interviews will depend to a large extent upon how well you can answer these questions.

Do you actually know as much about your chosen field as is expected of someone at your job level? Do you have an awakened perception of the present trends, the future outlook, and the history which has a bearing on these? Are you reasonably familiar with most of the important employers in your field and with some of the lesser known ones as well? How do they compare? What is the unique position of each? How old are they? How large or small are they? What is their financial standing? What are they best known for? What are they least known for? What are their newest plans?

Do you know as much as you should about the people in your field, the leaders and their lieutenants? What is their background and temperament? Why do you suppose they are in that field rather than another? What are their pet theories? What is their particular way of doing things?

Even if you don't have a lot of experience and are not looking for a top, policy-level job, you should know something about the head men in an organization, as their thinking and direction will apply to most everybody of consequence in that organization.

Finally, and most important, do you know enough about your particular prospects to talk with them about their organization and their problems, at least enough to lead with some intelligent, pointed questions about the way they do things?

If they are a commercial firm, exactly what do they manufacture or produce and precisely what services do they provide? To whom do they sell and in what size lots do they deliver? If they are a non-profit organization, exactly what purpose do they serve and what functions do they perform? Who supports them? How and why?

What are the policies and procedures of your particular prospects as differentiated from their competitors? Where would you fit into their existing set-up? What would your job with them be? What functions would you serve on that job? Whom would you work for? Whom would you work with? What help do they need, help which *you* could provide?

Look into the organizations which you already know something about. Investigate others with which you are not familiar. For practice pick a specified number in both the familiar and unfamiliar categories. Get some facts about them. Don't depend on guess work or hearsay.

There are four main channels through which you can get nearly all the information we're talking about.

1. Your friends can give you some of the answers if you choose the right people and ask the right questions.

2. Trade associations and professional societies can be very useful to you if you learn how to use them.

3. Newsstands are stacked high with clues if you recognize a clue when you see one.

4. Libraries are loaded with information for you if you know how to ask for what you want.

How to Get Helpful Information From
Friends and Acquaintances

To begin with, ask different friends so that you aren't misled by the single perspective of a small mutual admiration society. And be selective about whom you ask.

Many job hunters think they should see everybody who might, by remote chance, be of help. It's true that when it comes to tracking down specific job openings you should see everybody whom you suspect might know of a lead. But this does not apply to job research where you must pick your advisors with discrimination.

Before you solicit, or accept, help from a well-meaning friend, ask yourself, "What are his qualifications to help me and exactly what do I want him to do for me?" Does he have some useful information about the field in general or about a particular employer? Is he a person who would be pleased to give me that information or introduce me to someone else who could? Is he in a position to offer authoritative advice? Can he look into some important detail which is close to his fingertips and not otherwise readily accessible to me? Is he a good friend who might be willing to do a little detective work for me?

You might divide your friends, business acquaintances and other contacts into four categories, each one to a different role.

Campaign Strategists: The people who are established in an occupation, industry, or company of particular interest to you.

Deans: The elder statesmen in an industry, the people of stature and discretion to whom employers often turn for help in finding suitable new employees.

Detectives: The men and women who are in a position to ferret out specifics about a given company or a particular job. Among them are included previous employees of a company you'd like to join, a man in the bank which deals with that company, even a friendly receptionist. When you're seeking out helpful detectives, don't overlook the people who are served by the organization you're interested in. Sometimes the best way to get information about an apple stand is to ask the people who buy apples.

One of our Forumites recently applied for an executive position with a large trade association. The applicant had a number of contacts among the people who served at the association headquarters. But every time these people were queried about the subtle inner workings of the association they came up with evasive answers. It wasn't until the job hunter spoke with outside firms who were members of the association that he got the needed information. He found these association "customers" not the least hesitant to answer all the questions and volunteer their candid opinion of the association's needs. The applicant centered his job campaign around information gained from these latter sources and won the job.

This same technique can be applied to most any job in any field. Job hunters in the advertising agency field acquire revealing information about prospective agencies by talking with the clients who employ those agencies. Plant managers seeking new positions get a helpful inside look at potential employers by asking the people whom their prospects do business with. Applicants for editorial jobs gain significant information about individual publishers by talking with the writers who deal with those publishers. Even a purchasing agent once discovered a key job fact he needed by talking with the people who had been selling to the purchasing department of that employer.

Troops: Almost anybody who might have a bit of intelligence or news which will help complete your job research picture. The people at the Chamber of Commerce and local banks, old college mates, friends, and even a relative might be listed in this category. If your prospects are located in one of the smaller cities, you can find important details about them from people in various offices at the city or town hall.

Do not confuse the friends and acquaintances you turn to for research information with the ones you seek out for actual job leads. Save the job-lead contacts until your research has prepared you to go in there and sell your services rather than ask for a favor.

When you are seeking third-party contacts, be sure to brief the friend who is going to make that contact for you. If you don't, you're pretty sure to waste time and energy like this:

George is a good and well-meaning neighbor. He hears that you're looking for a new job and offers to introduce you to a friend whom he imagines may be of some help to you. He telephones this party and says, "Harry, I have a neighbor who's in the market for a job. He's a fine fellow, plays excellent bridge, and goes to church. His wife and mine are close friends. I'd appreciate it very much if you'd see him."

"I'd be glad to George," Harry replies. And he arranges to meet you at 11:30 Wednesday morning.

Now, if Harry is a friend of George's, Harry has almost got to see you for his friend's sake, not necessarily for your own sake. At this point the only things Harry knows about you are that you play bridge, go to church, and that your wife is a close friend of George's wife. Nevertheless, as he might be a good contact, you go to his office at the appointed time.

You and Harry talk about the weather, conditions in the Far East and that "gismo" he's got on his desk to distract attention. Harry's phone rings. His assistants run in and out of the office with "little matters" to clear up. His secretary makes strange signs at the doorway. Finally, if Harry is an especially good friend of George's, he takes you to lunch. If you're lucky, you'll be alone with him at lunch and have a chance to get to the subject of concern to you.

The minute you start talking, Harry realizes that your background and career interests are not what he had imagined they

were. In fact, he doesn't know a thing about your chosen field
or anybody in it.

On the sidewalk after lunch he shakes your hand, apologizes
for not being much help and wishes you good luck. And now
that it is established that there is nothing he can do for you, he
adds sincerely, "If there's anything I can do for you, don't hesitate to call on me."

In most instances your best personal friends actually know
very little about the work you do or your ability to do it. They
may know the name of the organization you work for and your
job title, but usually that's about all they retain. Consequently,
your friends either guess at what you do or, worse yet, try to
straighten you out about what you ought to be doing. So make it
perfectly clear to your friends what it is you do and what you're
up to now. Then you won't get your signals crossed.

When you arrange a good research interview be certain you
have some specific questions and requests ready before you go
in there. And don't come out till they have been answered one
way or the other. It's true the introduction may have been a
social one, but the interview is business.

Of course, you'll want to be polite, but your contact will
appreciate it if you get right to the point. Tell him what your
situation is and ask him point blank what you want from him.
If his response is evasive don't waste much time with him. And
watch out for those over-pleasant fellows who give freely of their
time but hem and haw when it comes to a specific favor. Cut
them short courteously.

You don't need a patronizing pat on the back. You need tangible help. And there are thoughtful men and women only too
glad to give you just that. Don't be shy about asking them.

Remember, there are few people who have not been on the
spot once or twice themselves in making a career decision or
job change. They know what's involved and there seems to be a
fraternal understanding. Also, they probably got where they are
partly because they weren't shy about making reasonable requests

of others. But you can't afford to limit your research completely to friends or to friends of friends or to friends of friends of friends. That sounds like a merry-go-round. And that's precisely what it will tun out to be if you try to depend entirely on whom you know.

How to Get Facts You Need From Trade and Professional Associations

There are hundreds of large, medium, and small trade and professional associations, societies, institutes, and clubs which are communication centers for the fields they represent. They have informative brochures, bulletins and news letters, edifying exhibits, conferences, seminars and closed-circuit television programs, as well as membership lists and directories.

Many of these are open or available for your inspection at little or no cost. Even when they are specified as being for "Members Only," a gentle knock on the door or a polite phone call will often get you inside. If that doesn't work, look around for a "member friend" who'll be glad to introduce you.

To find the associations in your field, look under "Associations" in the phone book of the nearest large city, or ask your reference librarian to show you a more complete and useful directory of the particular ones you are interested in.

As you look through these associations and societies, it might be helpful to divide them into two general categories. First, the associations whose membership is comprised of organizations in a given field. These are the ones most likely to be open to you. One of their purposes is to promote the industry they represent and they expect public requests for information.

The second category is that group of societies whose membership is composed of individuals in a particular trade or profession. These societies tend to be more private. Sometimes you can get good information from them but not always so easily.

In either case, the groups which can serve your purpose with facility are those which are large enough to have a headquarters office staffed by at least an executive director, often called "executive secretary." The only way you can check this detail is to phone or write them because some of the directory listings are no more than a telephone, or they are simply the address and phone number of the popular person who happens to be president for the year.

When you approach an association or society for research purposes, have specific questions ready. Write them out in advance. If you want general information: Would you like to see a brochure which describes their industry or do they have a movie of this nature? If so, when and where is the next showing? And would it be possible for you to see it?

Or if you want detailed information: Would you like to see programs of the last three annual conventions to discover the problems which were discussed and the names of the discussion leaders? Would you like to look at a list of the exhibitors at last year's trade show? Is there another exhibit scheduled soon? And would it be possible to get a guest ticket? Would you like to see their membership list with names and addresses or perhaps a more complete and informative directory? Do you want to know if Henry Stonnington will be one of the moderators at the eastern states forum on Thursday the 19th? And would there be any objection to your sitting quietly in the back of the room? Do you want to find out where John Wentworth went after he resigned as Assistant Sales Manager for the Ajax Company? Or do you want to know who took his place when he left?

Your questions must be business-like, sensible, and direct, if you want useful answers. You can't go to a trade association and ask them to tell you how to get a job. As you'll see in the next chapter, many associations do have some sort of actual job placement service; but that's not what you're after for the moment.

We are not trying to suggest that trade and professional associations are set up to supply you with job-finding information. In fact, they're not obliged to offer you any of the helps we've described. If you go to their headquarters or branch office, do not walk in and make demands. Just smile at the receptionist, and give her a chance to make helpful suggestions and to find your information in her files. Or possibly she will arrange for you to see the man who has all the information. You can afford to wait for this association man, as you know *he* has facts and access to things which can speed up your job campaign.

If you telephone or write, use the same tact and diplomacy. Try one or two questions at first. If you phone, make your first inquiry to the switchboard operator or receptionist. If you write, make your letter personal by finding the name of the executive director or one of his assistants from a library directory. And again wait patiently for the reply.

Remember that the answers are there. The association staff has them or can tell you where to get them. Our Job Finding Forum people gain reliable information from this source every day. Make a little extra effort. If the first association seems a little close-mouthed, go on to the next one or get an introduction from among your friends and contacts.

What to Look for on the Newsstand

Every newsstand has job-finding information for you. The big stands in major cities are stacked high with research facts about various occupations, careers, and potential job leads.

The Los Angeles Times or the *Seattle Post-Intelligencer* may carry a front page item about a new government contract issued to a nearby manufacturer. This manufacturer needs more people in various specialties and administrative capacities. One of them could be you.

The Detroit Free Press or the *Hartford Courant* may run a story about a major shake-up in a local industry. You might make yourself a part of this reorganization.

The New York Times or *Washington Star* may publish news about appointments of business and professional people. Between the lines, these announcements often mean new procedures and policies in the organizations represented. You could be a part of these changes.

Time Magazine or *U.S. News and World Report* may feature the biographical sketch of a key industrialist, social reformer, or professional man and the organization he's connected with. Information about his way of doing things could be a cue to finding out if he or a phase of his operation can use your help.

Fortune or *Business Week* may detail the story of a new pen manufacturer, its organization, its production plans, its sales plan, its purchasing methods, its advertising schemes, its distribution system. And they name the people who run these departments. You have a complete picture into which you might fit.

While you're reading this type of news, be on the lookout for the personal items, the new assignments, the resignations, the promotions, and personnel shifts from one organization to the next. Even the deaths and marriages of key people in the working world. As when a general manager dies, he is replaced by someone who may alter the operation and its staff. And when a business or professional woman marries, it can mean a change in the organization or department she runs.

We aren't suggesting you devote your job finding hours to the pursuit of social columns about betrothals. But a few of our Job Finding Forum people have found rewarding new positions by investigating the potential retirement of a key working-woman. This is a good example of the kind of imagination you can employ in using your newsstand as a source of job research.

Most news stories, features, and columns about the business and professional worlds suggest some sort of *change*, often a radical change which you might make yourself part of if you do a little research to find out what role you could play in the new arrangement.

One of the best means of pursuing your research further is following the trade and professional publications in your field. Their reporting often includes exactly the kind of detail you need. Read them from cover to cover and also between the lines, and keep reading every day until you get your job. Only a few trade papers and magazines are stocked by the large city newsstands. Many of them are distributed by subscription only. Some of these you'll find in the library. Others you may be able to get from a friend or acquaintance who subscribes.

You are almost certain to locate at least one of these publications concerned with your field or very closely related to it. If you are a regular reader of one particular trade journal, read it now more thoroughly than ever. But look at the others which aren't so familiar to you. They may offer a second perspective which can make a lot of difference in your approach to job finding.

These publications are more than just reading matter. Like the associations and societies, the trade and professional publications' offices are reference centers for their fields. They may prove an excellent source of information because they know everybody in their field regardless of club affiliation. And their files are usually arranged so that they can put their finger on some detail in a minute. In approaching these offices, follow the same general procedure suggested for the associations and societies. Don't forget that tact and diplomacy are keys through this door. If you run-up against some hard-to-find detail, you can very often discover it in a trade publication editorial office when all else has failed. And the information which you need usually isn't secret. Write a courteous letter. Or remember to smile prettily at the receptionist. She knows where the files are.

How to Use the Libraries

It would hardly seem necessary to advise an intelligent adult to look in the library for information. Yet we are continually surprised at the number of job hunters who bypass the library on their way to some other far less authoritative and informative source of facts. And those who do try the library don't seem to know how to look for what they want.

The big city libraries have industrial reference books, director-ies, and catalogues. They have handbooks, pamphlets, and folders of loose clippings. These collections are master keys to job finding and are usually gathered in one section of the library for easy accessibility. Sometimes you'll discover them in a separate corner of the general reference room, sometimes in a special room, and sometimes in a branch library near a place where that kind of reference is most frequently sought.

The smaller city libraries have a lot of this material or can tell you where to find it. And, in some rural areas, especially in the mid-west, there are excellent county libraries to which you can write and get both the information and some of the publications you are after by return mail. Then there are college and university libraries, and special business and professional libraries operated by various publications, by associations and by institutions.

Still other useful libraries are housed and run by large business and professional clubs and by individual companies. Obviously, the last are private. But in most instances, you don't need a pass-port to get in and you're welcome to study anything in the shelves and some of the things "underneath the desk."

From either a private or public library you can get the biggest part of what you need fast and easily not only because they have the information but also as they are staffed by experts trained and skilled to help you find it. Good librarians know how to search for things better than you do. If you approach them properly, you'll find that some of them know more about what's good for you than you know yourself.

The breadth and depth of the information you can get depends very much on you and the care you exercise in asking for what you want. You can't be too specific. And you can't be too general.

If you were to go to a grocery store and ask specifically for oranges, you might get the answer, "Sorry, we don't have any." And you would leave empty handed. But if you were to ask for breakfast fruit, the same clerk might suggest grapes, prunes or apricots, either of which would serve your purpose. And you could select one as you looked them over.

At the same time, if you were to make your request so general as to ask for "food," the storekeeper would hardly know where to start looking unless you carefully explained what you wanted it for and why.

This isn't as elementary as it sounds. Restless job hunters are notorious for fumbling such an important detail especially when they are in the early stages of deciding just what job they want.

So, before you go to the library, give some careful thought to describing your job-finding picture and research needs. Analyze it and propose your problem in simple language which will convey the same meaning to somebody else as it means to you.

Even if you're only looking for a specific detail and think you know exactly what book it's in, do not limit your inquiry to that book. The library may have a better reference for your purpose.

You may find that you can save time by taking a few minutes in advance to write your request or at least make some written notes more complete than a shopping list.

Whether you use libraries or other channels of information, when you begin to focus on specific potential employers, keep two basic considerations in mind: Under what kind of conditions and with what sort of people do you work the best? And what size organization is right for you?

These considerations may sound obvious, but your job satisfaction can depend on them. Don't take them for granted.

Of all the men and women who come to our Forums complaining that "office personality clashes" or "personal disagreements" are the reason they're looking for a new job, the vast majority would never have found themselves in this predicament if they had originally paid a little more attention to the kind of people they like to be with. Realize that in most instances you're going to spend as many hours with fellow employees as you spend with anybody for the rest of your working life. Be selective about the people you choose to work with if you want to enjoy your job.

Also the atmosphere of the office or buildings can have a lot to do with job contentment. If you thrive on action and excitement where telephones ring in a four-desk office and employees sprint up and down the halls, look for these characteristics in your prospective employers. If you prefer a little more peace and quiet, look for that.

You can sometimes glean a bit of this sort of thing from your research, especially from magazines and the more elaborate trade publications which illustrate their features with photographs of the personnel in the surroundings where they work.

When it comes to "what size organization is best for you," keep in mind that, if your qualifications and interests are broad and various, the small organization is usually best for you. Chances for advancement are excellent. And they offer about the same group benefits as large organizations. However, if your qualifications and interests are whittled to a pretty fine point of specialization, the large or fairly big organization is usually the right place for you. There are exceptions of course such as the fields of electronics and physics.

Above all, do not make the mistake of thinking that jobs in smaller organizations are the same except for the fact that things are done on a smaller scale. This is not true. The positions in the smaller operations are decidedly different jobs calling for different qualifications.

The production of a small manufacturing operation might be run by one man who is in charge of fabrication, finishing, quality control, and even packaging and shipping. The job applicant qualified for this position must have some experience in all these phases of the operation.

A larger manufacturer may be organized with one man in charge of fabrication and finishing, with a purchasing man doubling on quality control and with still a third employee running the packaging and shipping department. This narrows the qualifications for these jobs and calls for more experience in the specified areas.

The very large manufacturer is set up with one man heading fabrication, another finishing, another quality control, another packaging, and another shipping.

Where do you fit in your field? Be sure your research is sufficiently extensive to determine this or you're likely to be chasing one of those jobs which doesn't quite exist for you. Be very certain you have this worked out before you prematurely waste your time with a résumé or a wait in an unproductive employment line with other unlikely candidates who haven't bothered to investigate these essentials either.

As you continue with the next chapter on specific job lead sources, use the four main channels of information as we have suggested here.

Even if you think you have one or two good prospects on the fire, do not stand still waiting for the promised phone call or letter. Keep researching and you can't lose.

CHAPTER VII

Job-Lead Sources and How to Use Them

The ten major sources of job leads.
How to answer a classified ad.
Should you apply to the personnel department?
Should you seek help from a commercial employment agent?
Don't forget your former employer.

NATURALLY, you will use your own acquaintances to track down specific job openings. At this point, the only difference in procedure from the previous chapter is that you are looking for particular detail rather than general information. Now you know what you want. Don't make any bones about asking for it! Use as many friends and contacts as you have good reason to suspect might furnish specific leads for you.

Successful job hunters have gone so far as to use "club rosters" and "Christmas card lists" to make sure that anyone who might be helpful was not overlooked. Maybe you don't need to go through such an exercise, but realize that this is the time to tap every possible source and that it's very easy to overlook some of them without on orderly list to follow. And while you make up this list, don't forget your present employer or a previous one. Many of our Forum people have found their way to new jobs by reappraising an old or existing job situation and making a fresh approach to the same employer.

Understand that often you are like a grown-up child to an employer with whom you've been associated a long time. Though you are now of age, he still thinks of you as a greenhorn he knew "when." He imagines you have progressed some but he takes you pretty much for granted. He just isn't fully aware of what you have contributed and are presently contributing to his organization.

Perhaps he needs a reminder to help him visualize what you could mean to him in a new and greater capacity. One of the best reminders which you can give him is your new résumé with a job title that clearly shows what you want to do and with substantial evidence to show that you are qualified to do it. Leave it with him when you know he's got time to consider it thoughtfully. If you have two superiors who should know of your planned new direction, it's a good idea to let both of them see your new résumé at the same time. Don't dodge around or fret about the outcome simply because of company politics and personality clashes. If you think that there is more than an average amount of this going on, you would probably be better off elsewhere.

Follow up on more connections and friends. You can't afford to limit your new job search to *old* acquaintances when there are so many other excellent sources for job leads.

Sometimes it's a good idea to make early inquiry of employment services which you may have discounted because of some premature misconception or one or two unproductive experiences with them.

However, before you extend yourself by reaching far for a job lead, look around you. A lot of job hunters who have chased all over the place without results have eventually found just what they wanted through some previously unexplored source right in their own back yards.

Employment Helps Operated by Schools, Colleges, and Alumni Groups

You may not be a dedicated alumnus. But you may very well find a good new job through your college's placement bureau or alumni organization. Most college and university placement bureaus have job openings not only for the young graduates but also for alumni in mid-career. There is a certain species of old grad who invariably thinks first of his alma mater when looking for new employees for his firm. And a good many large corporations and organizations do a considerable amount of their recruiting on the campus and in the alumni offices. Some college employment services have been criticised for emphasizing the old-grad employer's needs rather than the job hunter's. Whether this criticism is valid or not, thousands of men and women do find excellent jobs through their college bureaus—and you should not overlook yours.

If you are a college graduate with an active alumni group in your area, check with them, too. They may have an informal word-of-mouth scheme for helping fellow-alumni job hunters, or a more organized procedure and full-scale service like the Career Planning Clinic which was for many years operated by the New York alumni from Notre Dame.

If your regional alumni group is large enough to have a club of its own, check the bulletin board. You'll find it most always has a few good jobs listed and one of them might be yours. If you are a woman, you may write to Catalyst Headquarters, 14 East 60th Street, New York, New York 10022. In addition to vocational guidance, this network of local resource centers sponsored mostly by colleges and universities conducts a job referral or placement service. Ask for their Roster Register Form. Fill it out and return it to Catalyst with your résumé of not more than two pages.

If you received your training at a professional or specialized school, remember that they, too, usually have employment exchanges both for the young grads and for those who have added some practical experience to their training.

Employment Information Available Through Business and Professional Clubs

Realize business and professional clubs which are large enough to have city headquarters or buildings of their own can be another good source of job openings. If any one of these clubs is large enough to have a library and a newsletter, it can handle inquiries from fellow members looking for employees. In many instances you don't have to be a member to avail yourself of such a source. Ordinarily, a polite letter to the president will be answered with a "Come visit us any time" reply. When you go there, see if they have a job placement bulletin board. You might find something of interest on it or they may be glad to list you.

Job Exchanges Sponsored by Local Civic Organizations

You can make inquiries at the local Chamber of Commerce or Junior Chamber of Commerce. In some cities, one or both organizations conduct a job exchange or a more complete service such as our own Job Finding Forum sponsored by the Junior Chamber in San Francisco. Perhaps the Chamber of Commerce in your area doesn't sponsor a service itself, but they can tell you who does.

If you feel that you have a specialized problem, such as a physical handicap or an environmental adjustment, you'll find special job-finding help through social and health agencies in metropolitan areas. Go to the library and ask for a directory of the ones in your vicinity. In New York, for example, there is a *Directory of Social and Health Agencies* put out by the Community Council of Greater New York and published by Columbia University Press. It has a whole section under "Employment and Vocational Counseling." You'll be surprised at the services available to special-situation job hunters at fairly high levels of professional and administrative experience.

State Employment Services

Whatever your past experience or personal feelings may be with respect to your State Employment Service, if you've crossed it off your list, you might consider it again. Many employers list their job openings with this government agency and lots of excellent jobs at moderate and fairly high salary levels are found through this source.

Like any government agency, there is red tape involved; and understandably, in an organization this size, there are always a few lesser skilled people. But the red tape isn't that involved and there are some very capable interviewers and clerks to help you to a good new job. Try your State Employment Service again. They do have interesting jobs, especially in the professional service departments of large city offices.

Employment Services Identified With Religious Organizations

Some individual churches in large cities sponsor excellent executive job exchanges with leads to professional and administrative positions at middle- and upper-income levels. A number of national religious-affiliated organizations are productive job sources at all income levels.

Outstanding among these are various agencies identified with the Jewish faith. Their services range all the way from vocational guidance to job placement. To find the service nearest you, write to the National Association of Jewish Vocational Services, 114 Fifth Ave., New York, New York 10011. This is a national coordinating office for practically all the Jewish affiliated agencies throughout the country. The group is knowledgeable, up-to-date, and well organized.

The Catholic church and various organizations connected with it sponsor extensive employment services. For example, you'll find Diocesan and Archdiocesan vocational and employment helps through the Chancery Offices in metropolitan areas across the nation. Local parish pastors can give you information on these or you may ask directly at the Chancery Office. When you inquire at a Diocesan Vocational Service, ask if they know of any other Catholic-identified organization which conducts career clinics.

Protestant-affiliated employment exchanges and helps are just as extensive as those organized by other denominations. But they are harder to find, for there is no central clearing house or information center. Use your imagination and be resourceful. Think of a Protestant-affiliated organization with which you are familiar. The Y.W.C.A. and the Y.M.C.A., for example, conduct all kinds of Employment Services in the large city areas. Some of them are excellent job-lead sources. Think of others and get in touch with them.

In considering religious-affiliated job-lead sources, do not conclude that they are services only for the lowest income brackets. Also realize that, except in rare instances, you do not need to be of the Protestant, Catholic, or Jewish faith to use these services. If you are a conscientious job hunter you will be welcome.

Placement Bureaus and Employment Services Administered by Trade Associations and Professional Societies

Trade and professional associations are among the most productive sources of new job leads. Some organizations conduct full-scale job-placement bureaus. Others have smaller job-exchange services. While still more have their own very informal means of offering you job-lead information.

Visit the library. Ask the reference librarian for a list of the the associations and societies related to your field of interest. Then write, phone, or visit each one on your list. Tell them what you want and ask them where you can get it.

One of the services of associations whose members are organizations is to help provide these organizations with employees. Their placement service or job lists are available to you. They might want to screen your résumé or possibly interview you first, but there's no charge involved.

When it's a society whose members are individuals in a given trade or profession, job-lead information which they have is usually marked "for members only." But files on these job leads are not locked in a secret vault and a friendly inquiry will generally get the information you want. If the society represents a field you have been in for a while, you probably know some of its members and can get an introduction.

While you're investigating these associations and societies, put some extra effort into tracking down their small subsidiaries and local independent clubs. These are indeed private societies, but, with a little polite prodding, you can usually find a friendly member who is pleased to give you some good dope on job leads.

Contact the headquarters of the large association and ask the information office if they know of any local groups in your area. If they do not, ask them to refer you to a regional affiliate which might be able to give you this information. Then inquire of this organization. They may have general information for you, but you need specifics: The name of the small group, where and when it meets, the address and phone number of its president or secretary.

Use every imaginable source to draw out these clues. The manager of the restaurant where the group meets will know the name of at least one group member with whom the restaurant deals. That's all you need. Call that member and he will tell you the club official who can give you more information regarding the group's activities. A program of their meetings and agendas will sometimes provide helpful employment ideas or they may have a regular single-fold newsletter or bulletin which includes a listing of positions available. These often contain some of the best job leads you can find in your field.

Help Wanted Advertisements and Classified Listings

Of course you'll study these advertisements in newspapers, but be sure also to investigate the ads in the trade and professional journals. And don't necessarily limit yourself to publications only related to your field, if the job you're after is a somewhat specialized service. For instance, if you are an accountant, don't confine your investigation to the accounting trade journals. Remember, *Foundry Management and Technology* runs help-wanted ads and so do *Advertising Age* and *The American Fruit Grower*. Use your imagination. Spend an hour or two in a large public or business library. Look through the trade papers and magazines.

again. You may be surprised at the job leads you can find this way.

Also, don't overlook the newsletters and bulletins put out by some of the smaller trade and professional groups. Employers who are hesitant to announce broadly a job opening are sometimes not at all reluctant to place a notice in papers whose circulation is limited to more select circles. These closed-circuit publications might also list you.

When you start looking at Help Wanted notices, you'll probably say to yourself regarding several of them, "I'm not exactly sure what that job is and whether or not I should follow it up." It takes a little practice to learn how to interpret these ads, and to read what lies between the lines.

Some sophisticated job hunters go through a painstaking procedure in looking through a large Sunday newspaper to cross-check the various announcements. Sometimes the same job will be advertised in the same publication on the same day by five different advertisers, the company itself, an employment agency, another employment agency, a management consultant firm, and possibly under still another lead in the business section. Cross-checking one against the other may give you information about the job which the first ad omitted, but this is a waste of energy unless you enjoy playing super-sleuth.

There are a few simple standards which you can employ to judge any ad by itself. The ads which are worth considering are specific, complete, and to the point. The ads which are a waste of time are vague, have an air of mystery about them, and seem contradictory in what they say.

The following are three samples of good ads for different jobs at different levels of experience. They are model ads, ideal from the job hunter's point of view. Ordinarily you won't find as many important details so clearly spelled out as they are here. Each one of these samples contains the *six basic essentials* that you should look for in any ad you wish to investigate. So, whether or not they pertain to your field, read them carefully, paying special attention to the six essentials illustrated in each one.

1. Job Title	*PUBLIC RELATIONS DIRECTOR*
2. Nature of Business	Multi-unit company in technical fields wants experienced director. Minimum 10 years corporate PR (5 years director or manager). Community relations ex-
3. Experience Sought	perience essential. Technical writing skill helpful. Newspaper background desirable.
4. Functions of Job	Must be able to create and execute corporate programs. Plan and control PR budget. Some public speaking. Work closely with top management.
5. Salary	Salary $30,000. Remuneration includes comprehensive benefits and moving expenses.
6. Firm Name and Address	FURROWS ENGINEERING CORPORATION Attn. J. C. Forsyther, Box 406 Redondo Beach, California 90277

1. Job Title	*ASSISTANT PRODUCTION MANAGER*
2. Nature of Business	To assist prod. mgr. in our fast-growing blouse division. Position requires man with proven ability to
3. Experience Sought	direct and coordinate all phases of manufacturing better blouses. Must have technical background to
4. Functions of Job	supervise production and maintain quality control from first pattern through finished product.
5. Salary	Salary $18,000. Send résumé and personal data to O. L. Reynolds
6. Firm Name and Address	"BEAUCHAMP" 720 Olive St. St. Louis, Mo. 63101

1. Job Title	*MORE THAN A SECRETARY!*
2. Nature of Business	Personable, mature young woman. Administrative ass't to President, small advertising agency. College,
3. Experience Sought	good at detail, some general knowledge of advertising, some typing convenient.
4. Functions of Job	Handle insertion orders, supervise direct mail assembly — liaison with free-lance artists and copy writers. Occasional client contact.
5. Salary	$12,000

6. Firm Name   COMMUNICATIONS, LTD.
   and Address   1195 Michigan Blvd. S.
                 Chicago, Ill. 60605

The six key elements in each ad are repeated here as a check list to use when you study ads which interest you.

_____ 1. Job Title

_____ 2. Nature of Business

_____ 3. Experience and Background Sought

_____ 4. Functions of the Job Advertised

_____ 5. Salary

_____ 6. Firm Name and Address

The above ads are prototypes, idealistic from your point of view. Few Help Wanted ads will include all six of the features illustrated.

With respect to Points 5 and 6, don't expect to find both the firm name and the salary offered in the same ad. However, the first ads which you answer in your campaign should specify one or both of these important details.

With respect to Points 1, 2, 3, and 4, you may not find them all listed or so clearly distinguishable in the ads which you investigate as they are in our samples. But once again the first ads you answer in your campaign should ordinarily contain at least two of these specifications.

Understand that these are rules of thumb for you to follow in selecting the ads which are most likely worth your answering.

We are not categorically stating that any ad which does not contain a majority of these points is not worthwhile. But be on guard if the ad doesn't come close to our specifications. Possibly it was deliberately written in a vague manner as a "come on," or maybe the employer is being perfectly honest. Perhaps he doesn't know what he wants or how to communicate what he wants.

Here are some other considerations to note in interpreting Help Wanted ads.

Steer clear of the ads with dramatic headlines—"Here Is the Chance of a Lifetime!" and "Rare Opportunity." The employer must be pretty hard put to get anyone to work for him if he has to resort to such display.

Look for incongruity in the copy. Beware the ad which glorifies a top-level position and then offers a starting salary which is decidedly below the job description level. Something is obviously off-base.

Be skeptical of the ads which say in essence that you start small but in six months you'll be a very important figure. Some employers are sincere and convincing about this. But no employer is actually promising more than the starting job title and salary. The rest is up to you.

Finally, if a job advertisement looks especially good but you don't have exactly the experience it calls for, do not eliminate yourself. If one or two of the requested specifications are missing from your background, you still may be considered a qualified applicant, especially if you are strong in the other respects. Just make sure that you do not accentuate the negative by apologizing for not having one of the qualifications called for. Don't mention it at all in either your letter or résumé.

Quite often the minimum requirements called for are only approximations, although it says "must." Employers specify maximums to protect themselves from a deluge of applications from people who are below the level or off to one side.

When an employer has an urgent need for someone to help him, you'll get the job if you are able to convince him that you can do it better than anybody else in the employer's price range. As often as not some of the details he sets forth in his original specifications turn out to be forgotten technicalities unless it's a very large corporation recruiting an army of new employees.

When you find an ad to which you'd like to reply, write a letter and enclose a résumé regardless of what the ad tells you to do. A good ad gives you everything you need to work with: the job title, the functions, and even some background which suggests types of problems you would face on that job.

It's simple. Just adapt your résumé and master letter to these specifications. At this point you need not worry over any additional details requested. For instance, if the ad reads: "State salary and availability," you can forget it for the time being, if you wish to. Your purpose is to influence employers. It is to get your foot in the door and to get an additional response that will give you more information upon which to base your second step. And nothing will get your foot in the door as surely as a business-like, straight-forward résumé without addenda having to do with your personal background, availability, and salary demands.

Some people have found jobs through Situation Wanted advertisements. However, we have known so many persons who try to find positions through Situation Wanted ads with no results at all, that we can't recommend your spending money this way.

The basic idea of a Situation Wanted ad is the shotgun approach. Far less effective than a rifle shot aimed at a predetermined target, it usually becomes a lazy job hunter's attempt to avoid making his own decisions and to by-pass the chore of job research, two essential elements of a successful campaign. There *is* such a thing as an effective Situation Wanted ad, but this can be prepared only by first doing those things which a person using this approach is generally trying to avoid; that is the making of one's own decisions and the carrying out of one's own research.

Ordinarily it is not enough to advertise your general background in a place where you're hoping some customer might see it and figure out for himself some way in which he might use it. Also, selecting the right publication for your particular ad is something of a specialized skill in itself. It is useless to speculate on this or follow a hunch as it takes a kind of experience you probably don't have.

If you decide to take a long shot on a Situation Wanted ad, try to include the same elements that were illustrated in the Help Wanted advertisements and notices. Be as specific as possible about your qualifications and, above all, do not be vague about the organizations which you have worked for and about the kind of a job you want now.

The Direct Approach to the Employer or Personnel Department

Before you consider employment agencies, placement bureaus, and other independent recruiters, realize that their only consequential advantage to you lies in the fact that the good ones have their fingers on the market or on specific job openings. If you have time to research the market yourself, you'll find that you can dig out the job openings on your own.

Many employers use agencies and other types of personnel search specialists to save themselves time and effort in finding and screening applicants. Even so, you are perfectly free and welcome to query or apply directly to almost any employer who will then see that your application is given full consideration. What is more, if you have done a good job with your research, résumé, and letters, you, yourself, have already done a large part of the screening for the employer.

"To what department in a given organization do you make application?"

You may question whether, at your level, you should direct an initial query to the personnel department. The answer is probably "No," for the following reason.

From one organization to the next there is a considerable variation in personnel departments. In one instance, the company personnel office is nothing more than a routine clerical clearing section to which nobody "inside" or "outside" seems to pay much attention. Obviously, you waste time in approaching such a department. In another instance, "personnel" may be a key department in the organization, and the director and his assistants do practically all the recruiting and hiring; so the personnel people have a great deal of influence. They form the policies and sometimes they have the final "say" about who goes to work for that organization and who does not.

But, even if you are applying to an organization with a strong personnel section, it is usually best to address your initial communication to the department where you think you can serve— so long, of course, as you make your communication tactful and are not obviously trying to pull some trick to bypass somebody. If you are tactful in this way, you do stand a chance of attracting the attention of someone who is directly interested in you and he might so indicate his feelings when he passes the matter on to personnel for their consideration and follow-up.

Now, which individual in a selected organization is the right one to address? One rule of thumb is to apply to the president if it's a small to medium-sized organization, the executive vice president if it's a medium-sized to fairly large firm, and to the department head or division vice president if it's a very large concern.

Be careful not to write to the man or woman at your same level or the one whom you might possibly replace. If you have any doubt about the proper level to approach in any organization, go at least one step higher than you had planned, even though this may be to the president himself. For purpose of illustration, we suggest that even if you are looking for a job as errand boy you might address your application to the president or chairman of the board. If the top official won't handle your case, he will pass it down, possibly with a nice memo, to the people who *will* handle it. And anything which gets handed down with a memo from the head office usually gets attention.

We are not being facetious about this. We have known office boys who got jobs as a result of direct application to the president of good-sized organizations. And, by addressing the head man, you have nothing to lose.

Thousands of job hunters turn almost automatically to commercial employment agencies after personal contacts have been exhausted. At the same time, contrary to a popular opinion, only a small percentage of job finders actually get jobs through this source. But commercial agents *are* a possible road to job contacts and you might do well to try some reliable ones if you understand how to use them to your advantage.

There are hundreds of them. They are licensed and controlled by the laws of the state and sometimes the cities in which they operate. Additionally, in some localities, they are required to file bonds and live up to the standards of the bonding companies. In most states the licensed agencies are not permitted to charge you an advance fee for any service. In other states, where advance fees are permissible, a small registration fee of ten dollars is all you should have to pay. The principal charges of all commercial employment agencies are scaled to a percentage of the salary of the job to which they lead you if, and only if, of your own free will, you decide to accept the job. The fee is payable after you're on the job.

While the law is quite rigid with respect to the fees these people can collect, the actual service you get from one agency to the next can vary considerably.

First, almost all commercial agents work primarily for the *employer*. Regardless of whether you or the employer pays for the service, the professional contact man is primarily concerned with the *employer's* welfare and good will, which isn't necessarily yours. It's a pretty good idea to keep this in mind throughout your dealings with anyone who is paid for bringing employer and employee together, no matter how legitimate and highly reputable your middle man may be.

Whenever a professional agency man seems to be pushing you to take a particular job, ask yourself, "Who is he favoring—the employer or me?" Ideally, of course, the answer should be "both of you." But frequently it's one-sided—for the other side. A lot of job hunters have been seriously misguided, lacking this insight into the agent-employer relationship.

Second, the commercial employment agents are suposed to have a practical knowledge of jobs, job specifications, and particular job openings. Indeed, the established and reputable agents do know their job market and are well equipped to advise you with respect to it. But that's all.

With few exceptions, they are not career guidance counselors, although many of them purport to be—and they do not have the training or educational qualifications to advise you regarding the kind of work you should be doing or can do. The only things which they are equipped to appraise are your personality, your appearance, and your record of employment. They do not know what your aptitudes or vocational interests are, and they do not know what makes you tick. They do not know the personal circumstances and other subtle motivating factors which have a decided bearing on your career and job preferences. You're in danger when you let the ordinary employment agent guess at these things and advise you according to his speculation.

Understand that it is the agent's or recruiter's assignment to find people with special experience to fill particular jobs. To function efficiently, in most circumstances, he must conform to certain specifications. If your particular background doesn't conform to these specifications in every respect, he may cast you aside as unqualified or twist you around to fit into a spot where he thinks he can sell you at the moment. Even some of the free-service placement bureaus, with the best intentions and without any exchange of money, will try to do the same thing.

If an agent tells you that you're hopelessly out-of-step or tries to veer you off in a direction away from your pre-determined goal, realize that his principal frame of reference is that list of job openings which he has at the moment. To be sure, that list is pretty realistic. But it is not the only list, and it is not necessarily the list with your job on it. If several different agents tell you the same disconcerting story, it is no cause for concern because different agents often have about the *same* list, particularly when they are agents who specialize in one or two occupational fields.

We are not suggesting that the agents or recruiters are wrong. But like everyone else, they have their limits. So don't worry if they give you a hard time, especially if your situation is out of their normal sphere.

If you have worked out each step of your campaign carefully and have been honest with yourself, you probably have a much better idea of where you belong than they do. Don't change that idea just to suit the convenience of some employment agency, placement bureau, or company recruiter.

Selecting the individual agencies which are best suited to your needs is pretty much a matter of playing by ear. But a little system on your part will save a great deal of time and energy.

To begin with, before you burn shoe leather chasing around and strain your wrist from cramming your life history into the too-small spaces of endless application blanks, get yourself a directory of the agencies in your area. Often a Sunday newspaper which has a large Classified Ad and Business Opportunities section, offers a free directory of the better agencies. This booklet will be sent to you on request. Keep it at hand for reference while you're going through the job listings in the paper.

Consider the following things when you select an agency.

Size: There are a large number of small agencies, some of which are only a one-man operation. There are also a small number of large agencies, some so big as to be departmentalized.

The large agencies have ordinarily been in the business longer and are more solidly established in the occupational fields which they represent. The big ones are probably better for you if you have an orderly background of progress and accomplishment in a given field and if you wish to continue in pretty much the same line of work. If this is not the case, however, they won't generally do much for you. In fact, some of them won't even consider your application. Most of the big ones are more like mass production, order takers rather than creative salesmen.

If you are making a consequential change in your occupation or if you have relatively little work experience, pick a small agency which will take the time to give you and your situation individual attention. In selecting a small one, the address and the appearance of its office does count for something. Don't expect a luxurious office suite, but watch out for those dingy, second-floor hall closets. Don't "Walk In" as it says on the door. Stay out. If you're not sure from the outward appearance, you might step inside. Let what you observe in two minutes determine whether you want to stay long enough to fill out another blank and take the time to wait for another interview.

The Number to Use: Quality is what you're looking for and a dozen agencies should be ample. If you have to go beyond that number, you'll find the same jobs coming up and you'll get the same story from one agent to the next. Few employers who use agencies stick exclusively to one. No matter what you are told to the contrary, it's rare to find a close marriage between a legitimate employer and one agency. Consequently you're unlikely to miss out on something by limiting your selection to the twelve agencies. In fact, if your search for a job resolves itself into chasing around after an endless number of employment agencies, you are short somewhere in the basic preparation of your campaign.

Specialization: There aren't many employment agencies which turn down the employer's requests to fill a job in any field. However, a lot of the better agencies are specialized or are divided into separate departments. This is important to you because those which specialize in your field are better versed in it—and knowledge of job openings in your particular field is the thing which you pay an agent for.

The Male and Female of It: If you have a personal prejudice against woman's place in the working world, this is not the place to exercise it. There are both men and women in employment agency work. Don't get your dander up if some people aren't overpolite and gracious in receiving you, for they do have to interview hundreds of job hunters, many of whom aren't the easiest people in the world to talk to. Some agents are inclined to be a little critical and brusque. But don't let this throw you.

Very often these agents are really in there pitching to find a good job for you. And that's all you're after.

At the same time, when you go to an employment agency, you offer them a chance to make money on your exprience and capabilities. If you get the feeling that you're being treated badly, get out of there. The agency next door has the same job openings for the same fee and will probably treat you courteously.

Management Consultants Concerned with Executive Recruiting and Personnel Search

If your annual salary is close to twenty thousand dollars or better and if you have a fairly consistent record of employment, you will do well to investigate management consultant firms. Most of them recruit personnel to fill their clients' needs in addition to providing other services. Others specialize in this personnel search activity.

They are paid entirely by their clients; so there is no charge to you. And they are easy to find. The American Management Association has a four-page paper titled "Executive Recruitment Organizations" which is free for the asking. Beyond this, the AMA publishes an extensive *Directory of Consultant Members* which you can purchase for three dollars. To get either of these publications, write the Publications Sales Department, American Management Association, 1515 Broadway, New York 36, N.Y.

Another good reference for locating this type of recruiter is the membership list of the Association of Executive Recruiting Consultants. Though a relatively small group, its standards are high and its members are reputable. The AERC is harder to find because they have no permanent headquarters and their officers change from year to year. Check with the business libraries and the Chamber of Commerce to get their present address. The AERC will send you their membership list without charge.

Not listed on any of the previously-mentioned rosters are a good number of very small independent consultants who specialize in executive recruiting. You'll have to do a little digging to find the dependable ones in your area. Again check with the local Chamber of Commerce and other business associations in your immediate vicinity.

Some of the smaller consultants and private practitioners do not necessarily limit their activity to the twenty-thousand-dollar-and-above job categories. They have good job openings for less. You don't need any special introduction or other eligibility qualifications to apply to executive recruiters for a job opening. Simply send them a copy of your résumé along with a covering letter describing your interests and, perhaps, personal background.

These people have too many applications to interview all their applicants personally, but they will review your material conscientiously and give you an honest reply. If they tell you they'll "file your résumé for future reference," they mean it. They will. And you may hear more from them shortly if they tell you so. However, a number will move your résumé into an inactive file unless you remind them occasionally that you are still actively looking.

There is a lot of job locating by these consultant firms. Some have job openings in as many as eighty categories. You can't afford to overlook them if you've had reasonably substantial experience. Just remember that they work for their clients, the employers, and not necessarily for you. Keep this in mind and handle it according to your own judgment.

When an executive recruiter is interested in you, he may want to revise or help rewrite your résumé in a chronological form. There is no charge for this, though be careful that the rewriting does not alter the basic course which you have previously determined. Stick to your own career decisions.

Now you have a guide to ten major sources of job leads.

Here they are repeated as your working check list.

1. Employment helps operated by schools, colleges, and alumni groups

2. Employment information available through business and professional clubs

3. Job exchanges sponsored by local civic organizations

4. State employment services

5. Employment services identified with religious organizations

6. Placement bureaus and employment services administered by trade associations and professional societies

7. Help-wanted advertisements and classified listings

8. The direct approach to the employer or personnel department

9. Commercial employment agencies

10. Management consultants concerned with executive recruiting and personnel search

Some of the above may be more suitable to your needs than others, but investigate all of them and check them off as you go along. Add others of your own if you like. You have not done justice to yourself or your job-finding campaign until you have made an inquiry into every source on this list. So refer to your library, get out your telephone book, and prepare to write letters.

CHAPTER VIII

Why Bother With a Résumé?

You are counting on friends and connections.
You believe your experience doesn't fit a résumé.
You think it's ostentatious.
Or you think you are on too high a level.

Perhaps you don't feel that a résumé is necessary for your particular job-finding campaign, and you have what seem perfectly logical reasons for feeling this.

You are counting on your many good friends and business acquaintances who don't need a résumé to help you.

Your kind of experience doesn't reduce itself well to a precise, descriptive form.

It's not good taste to boast of your achievements in such an ostentatious manner.

Résumé writing is too elementary for a person at your level.

Examine your objections, one at a time.

You Are Counting on Friends and Business Acquaintances

You are a job hunter with excellent business contacts and well-situated friends who are anxious to offer helpful suggestions and to arrange introductions and interviews for you. These people know you and your good reputation. It hardly seems necessary to give them a résumé to verify it.

However, experience shows that ordinarily your best friends don't understand just what you do and can do for a living. So how can these people who are guessing at your job qualifications and interests be expected to help place you in a lasting job? Your friends are less likely to mislead you if you provide them with a clearly stated résumé as a guide. Give them a few extra copies to facilitate their efforts.

If you're counting to any extent on "Whom do you know," your second consideration must be "How many do you know?"

Let's say that you belong to some trade or professional societies. Maybe you are in a luncheon club. Your associates from any one of these organizations might make up a cadre to start your job finding going. But they'll never add up to the support you need to wage a full-fledged job-finding campaign.

You need more contacts than just these friends or business associates. And you must meet new people who don't know you at all. These persons are far more likely to help you find what you want if they learn about your background from a factual résumé rather than from a second-hand, word-of-mouth report.

Your Kind of Experience Isn't Adaptable to a Resume

You may have been in "secret" government work and are restricted in what you can say. Your experience may have involved complicated team operations so that it's impossible to distinguish what you alone accomplished. Your field may be in some phase of creative art which can't be defined in résumé form. Actually, however, the only kind of experience which can not be described to advantage in a résumé is no experience.

If you have been in any sort of confidential work you are, of course, limited in describing what you did. But you are probably not prohibited from indicating how well you've done. Usually you can employ some facts and figures which show results from your efforts. In almost every instance, it is possible to use quotes of commendation from authoritative sources to project your capabilities.

If your work has involved a complicated team activitiy and you served with this group for a consequential length of time, you must have contributed something specific to it. What was your role? That's what your prospective employer wants to know. If you insist that it's impossible to single out your individual contribution, you can at least relate what the team accomplished and identify yourself with the results.

If you are in one of the creative or artistic fields it is true that final proof of your ability may be in your sample case rather than in a résumé. But how do you get inside to demonstrate this?

To introduce yourself to new and better prospects it takes more than a phone call or a friendly letter. A good résumé is the answer, and it's entirely possible to pin-point your particular kind of talent in résumé language, i.e., in terms of measurable results.

Look at your work objectively from the point of view of your employers and customers. Probably some recognized authority thought highly of your work. What did he say about it? Quote him. Somebody paid you and benefited from your efforts. How did they benefit? Do a little research on your own work. Go back to your former employers. They can help you dig out tangible results from your efforts. Here is a sample of proof-positive results which one artist found by returning to a former employer.

"Last year, I redesigned, from cover to cover, the annual Crochet Book published by a leading woman's magazine. This newly designed booklet sold 66% more copies, at 75% more per copy, than it had ever sold in its seven years as an annual publication."

If you are a sensitive artist, it may seem like blasphemy to measure a piece of creative work in numbers. But commercial employers think in terms of business. Nothing will get you an audience to review your samples faster than a résumé which specifies financial results.

You Believe It's Bad Taste to Boast of Your Achievements

You are a decent sort of person hesitant to show-off your accomplishments in a résumé. But business is business. Everybody who is anybody advertises himself and continues to advertise himself in one way or another.

There is no more legitimate way for you to do this than through the medium of a factual résumé. It is accepted as standard in just about every sort of business and in very many professional occupations. As far as boasting is concerned, you will see that a good résumé does not include personal opinions. It simply states the facts.

You Think Writing a Résumé Is Too Elementary for You

You are well-advanced in your career and believe that résumés are only for younger job seekers. But no matter how much experience you've had, you probably have had very little to do with the specialized skill of packaging and selling yourself. Most likely you have a lot to learn about how to translate your experience into benefits for a prospective employer. The best way to learn how to do this is to organize your selling points and write them in a résumé. If you do a good job of it, you'll see for yourself what an advantage it is.

Whatever other prejudices you may have against résumés, realize that the fellow who's after the same job which you want probably already has a résumé in circulation. Maybe you and he will be brought up for consideration at the same time by one of your preferred prospects. If that prospect has a good résumé from your competitor and only a word-of-mouth account about your background, you could end up out of luck—and only because the employer didn't have a written reminder of your qualifications in front of him at the moment. This happens, especially when an employer needs help in a hurry.

If you have already tried to work out a résumé without results, it's probably either because you wrote the wrong kind of résumé for your particular needs or because you didn't write it well. So begin anew. Follow the suggestions in the next two chapters. They will help you decide what kind of résumé you need and show you how to write it simply and clearly.

CHAPTER IX

What Kind of Résumé Is Best For *You*?

**An "original idea" résumé? A chronological résumé?
A functional résumé? A combination?**

Some job hunters prepare a conservative, chronological listing of their past employers, giving names and dates without any further elaboration. This document is typed formally, marked "Confidential," and reproduced for general distribution.

These people feel it's advisable to hold fast to dignity. They trust that such a factual record of employment, showing that they have held good positions in previous jobs, will locate them another good job.

Other job applicants work out complete brochures about themselves and concoct all sorts of gimmicked-up résumés. They are opportunity seekers who believe it's a good idea to throw a brick through the prospective employer's window to get his attention.

These are opposite extremes of which you can't afford to be either.

If you are one who believes a dignified listing of dates and employers' names will speak for itself, be advised to the contrary. It is, of course, important to mention names of some past employers, especially if they are good names. But it is what you did for them and what resulted from your particular efforts on their behalf that counts for a great deal more than the names themselves and the length of time you were associated with them. It is important that your résumé be more interesting than a list of names and dates.

You would appreciate this if you'd ever had to struggle through a hundred résumés looking for the one man or woman you need. While a list of dates and names might bring back memories to you—and from your point of view be a revealing mirror—such a document, by itself, does not project very much of an image of you to your prospective employers. No matter how established and well-known your past employers might be, you cannot camouflage your name behind theirs and expect yours to stand out. First and foremost, it is you you're talking about in your résumé. You must step forward and speak for yourself—in very precise language—if you want to be selected from the crowd.

Now, if you are one who suspects that a brochure-like or gimmicked-up presentation of your experience and background will distinguish you from the average applicant, realize that even if you do command some initial attention with such a device, the employer will usually conclude that you must be hard pressed for a job to go to all that expense and trouble. This sort of thing has been tried so many times before that no matter how original you are, you run the risk of appearing as an imitator.

Through the years at our Job Finding Forum we have seen a good number of beautifully prepared, slick brochures, some of them reproduced in color with appropriate headlines and copy describing the applicant's claims and illustrated with photographs. Many job hunters have used the recognizable format of a magazine, such as *Time*, and adapted their experience to its familiar headings. Others have printed up a newspaper-like article describing their experience and circulated these clippings to prospective employers. Still others have used a book format, complete with jacket. And résumés like film strips and television story-boards come a dime a dozen in the advertising business.

We have seen résumés on colored paper with another colored ink, résumés prepared with free-hand lettering, résumés sealed in fancy plastic coating and a hundred and one other tricky devices. But we rarely see any of them get a job!

One young man came to us recently with his idea of an

attention-getting résumé. It was a perfectly regular résumé, but at the top of the first page he had glued a miniature, three-dimensional hammer hitting a little nail. Immediately beneath it was the caption: "Here's an applicant who hits the nail on the head!" Obviously it hadn't "struck" any employers that way or he wouldn't have come to us.

Another opportunity-seeking salesman arrived for the first time at our Forum loaded down with extra copies of a résumé which he distributed to everybody at the meeting and, to assure complete coverage, he gave one to the janitor and two to the watchman. The entire first page of this résumé was a big photograph of a well-curved and sparsely-clothed young female. We all agreed she made a delightful picture.

A caption at the bottom read:

This is my wife! It took a good education, some substantial experience, and a lot of perseverance to make her mine.
I can sell your prospects with these same qualifications.
Turn the page and see for yourself.

This man got interviews all right—several of them, in fact. He also got a good number of letters in response But no job. Most of the men who responded were curiosity seekers looking for a chuckle, not an employee.

There are fundamentally two kinds of résumés: the old chronological-type résumé and the more modern functional-type résumé.

The chronological résumé is, of course, the one in which you outline your work history with the hope that some as yet unidentified employer will find something in your past which he can use now. This is the résumé which ordinarily itemizes "when" and "where" you've been and offers some general information about your "duties" and "responsibilities." Its familiar format looks like the following résumé of a young design engineer.

Glance through this one whether or not it happens to apply to your field or experience level. For our purposes here, the applicant could just as well be an interior decorator or a public relations man. So don't be concerned about the technical nomenclature or the fact that the author may not be your age. Just review it for clarity and salesmanship.

Can you find the *man* and his capabilities? Does he sound steady and consistent like a person with convictions? Imagine that you are a busy employer with thirty-two résumés on your desk. You need a young man who can take responsibility, can get things done in a hurry, and, finally, one who will work cooperatively with the rest of your team. Would you take the time to interview this man on the strength of his résumé alone? Or would you go on to the next résumé because this one leaves too many questions unanswered?

RÉSUMÉ
OF

Thomas Huld
12 Garfield Road
Tuckahoe, New York 10707

U.S. Citizen	Age 37	Married, 2 Children
Height 5'10"	Weight 175 lbs	Health Excellent

Education: Polytechnicum, Munich, Germany. Degree in Mechanical Engineering. Post Graduate work at Worcester Polytechnic Institute, Worcester, Mass.

1971 to Present: New York Engineering Company, Inc. Chief Designer, hydraulic presses and equipment. Duties include supervision of two lead men and design groups.

1966–1971: Baxter, Inc., Worcester, Mass. Lead man of design group. Reported to Section Supervisor Mr. Harold Reading. Responsible for detail designing and calculation of all-welded frames for hydraulic presses, cylinders, control devices, pistons, etc.

1965 (8 months): Brooklyn Iron & Steel Corp. Welder

1965 (4 months): Mason Motors (Ford Agency) Mechanic

1964–1965: Süddeutsche Maschinenbau Gesellschaft, Germany (one of the largest European hydraulic press manufacturers). Junior engineer on detail design of die-spotting presses and special equipment.

1960–1964: Summer Jobs and Apprenticeship. Hand molding in a German iron foundry. Training in autogenous electric and gas welding. Maintenance and repair, steam engines & boilers.

Military service—Navy, destroyer escort. Fireman, greaser, and Assistant Engineer. Honorable Discharge.

Now, compare that résumé with the one which follows. The next one is an entirely different kind of résumé prepared by the same man. This is a sample of the functional-type résumé. It starts out with a specified job title which indicates that the applicant knows what he wants to do. Then, as you can see, the résumé continues to describe only that part of his experience which applies to the particular job at stake. Significantly, the functional headings are listed in the order of their importance to the employer rather than in the order of the job hunter's past history.

Glance through this résumé. Don't be concerned about the technical terms. And again, imagine that you are a busy prospective employer. Does this résumé sound like that of a steady man who knows where he's going, who can accept responsibility, who gets things done well and fast, and who will cooperate with his associates? Wouldn't you separate this résumé from the rest of the pile and call the applicant for an interview?

Thomas Huld
12 Garfield Road
Tuckahoe, New York 10707
914-963-3077

DESIGN ENGINEER—Hydraulic Presses and Equipment

Directing and Supervising Design

As chief of Designers for the New York Engineering Co. since 1971, I have supervised 8 men in detail designing and calculating on hydraulic presses up to 2000 tons capacity.

For example, one project was the remodeling of a stretch form machine to handle a greater capacity, to operate more efficiently and at less cost with fewer operators.

We designed a re-enforced machine for a 20% load increase; a motor-driven instead of hand-operated adjustment device; a streamlined machine body to house controls; and an automatic control device to make the machine independent of the operators' skill.

As in many other instances, this assignment was a rush order. The design was completed approximately 3 weeks ahead of schedule and the manufactured machine has been in use for about 3 years with only minor servicing and repairs.

Designing

My 5 years as a draftsman for Baxter, Inc., Worcester, Mass. included work on hydraulic equipment, controls, and circuits. For instance, I designed a pneumatically-operated ram locking device for a die-spotting press which could be installed as a complete unit, thus cutting down installment costs 30%. For another project, I designed a hydraulic circuit to operate moving work tables. This device has been adopted as standard and Baxter has sold over 1000 of these circuits.

Background

I received my early experience with Süddeutsche Maschinenbau Gesellschaft, one of the leading European manufacturers of hydraulic presses. I worked with design problems involving high pressure seals up to 5,000 pounds per square inch. My apprenticeship included practical experience with hand molding in an iron foundry; in autogenous electric and gas welding; in boiler maintenance.

Education

M.E. Degree. Honor graduate. Polytechnicum, Munich, Germany. Post-graduate work. Worcester Polytechnic Institute.

Personal

Age 37. Married, 2 children. Member A.S.M.E.

You can see that this functional résumé is more directly to the point and leaves less work and speculation up to the employer.

Now, look through it again for the following key features:

To begin with, the young designer has eliminated superfluous personal statistics, some of which, incidentally, emphasized his foreign origin which he felt was a big strike against him.

In the second place, the applicant has removed a lot of confusing dates which appeared so frequently that he looked as if he were an unreliable job hopper. Also he has moved his employers' names from top billing to a position where they are an integral part of the story about Thomas Huld.

Thirdly, our friend has completely omitted some of his past jobs and de-emphasized others which have little or nothing to do with the job he's after now.

Finally, and most importantly, the applicant has added some descriptions which illustrate exactly what he has done. They specify breadth and depth of his experience measured in *numbers* like "New York Engineering Co. since *1971*," "supervised 8 men," "presses up to *2000* tons capacity," "high pressure seals up to *5000* pounds per square inch." And the descriptions point to some *results* which are also measured in *numbers* like "3 weeks ahead of schedule," "3 years with only minor servicing . . .," "cutting down installment costs *30%* . . . "

These are important features which can make all the difference with respect to whether or not a résumé leads to an interview.

Of course, it's possible to incorporate some of these with other vital ingredients into a chronological résumé. There are circumstances when a modified chronological résumé may get the results you want.

A modified chronological résumé may suit your needs if your jobs have progressed in a logical order, if those jobs have been fairly much in the same general field, if you have had relatively few jobs, each for a substantial length of time, and if you want to proceed in just about the same line of work.

That's a lot of "ifs." But some job hunters can meet all those conditions favorably. Perhaps you can. If so, you may be scarce enough to be in demand and don't need a functional résumé. However, no matter how great the demand is for people with your qualifications, you are still in competition with others for the best jobs. So if you decide on a chronological résumé, make certain that it's an improvement over a mere listing of dates, names, and duties. Turn to the Appendix for a sample modified chronological résumé. There, you will find the things which the employer wants to know about you. Incorporate them in your chronological résumé. They will make your application more interesting and persuasive.

You can be more certain of winning, however, with a full-scale functional résumé. In the beginning, it will take a little longer because you have to search your market carefully, appraise your assets more realistically, and pinpoint your own goals. But the functional résumé will probably save you weeks, maybe even months, in the long run. Time and again well-qualified persons in our Job Finding Forums have lost weeks and months trying in vain to penetrate the job-finding "front" with a chronological résumé. When they started anew with a strong functional résumé, they got the job they wanted.

Ask yourself, "Exactly for what purposes are you writing a résumé? What function will it serve? How will you use it?"

One purpose, of course, is to call an employer's attention to you so that you can get an interview. In most circumstances, that is as far as any job-finding document will get you. Employers seldom have occasion to order employees by mail. They like to see them first.

That's where the second and more important purpose of writing a good résumé comes into play. The practice you get in *writing* about yourself prepares you to *speak* for yourself in interviews when you must talk at your best. If you work hard preparing a good functional résumé, when you get to the interview you'll *sound* like the man for the job.

When you prepare only a chronological résumé without investigating the employer's needs in advance, you walk into the interview without knowing anything much about the employer. Yet he knows some things about you from your résumé. This tends to make the interview a one-sided affair with the interviewer in control.

But when you work up a functional résumé, you have to

familiarize yourself with the employer's needs first. Then, when you come to the interview, you know nearly as much about him as he knows about you, and you are prepared to talk about him and his needs. Most employers appreciate a two-sided interview because they can get to the point faster and easier.

Many uninitiated job hunters raise the objection, "If I restrict my résumé only to that part of my experience which applies to one particular kind of job, I have to leave out some other experience which the employer might be able to use." That is true. But by expanding into detail about all of your experience in a résumé, you run the risk of sounding as if you were all over the lot. When you claim that you can do a lot of different things, you automatically suggest that you may not be able to do any one thing well. In this age of specialization, people are likely to be hired primarily because of "a certain something," not because of a whole lot of little things.

The specified job title at the top of your résumé clearly indicates a single purpose and sense of direction. This kind of personal conviction on your part, by itself alone, has as much "sell" in it as anything which you can project to a prospective employer. Ironically enough, even if he's not looking for someone to fill that exact position, he is more likely to interview you than he is when you send him a chronological résumé of your life history and challenge him to find something in it which he can use.

You can expand on other phases of your experience and interests after you get into the interview if it seems desirable. Contradictory as it may seem, many of our Forum people who have managed to get a "foot-in-the-door" with a specified job title have wound up working for that employer in another somewhat different capacity. But it was the functional résumé with the proclaimed job title which got them inside.

The majority of employers will welcome your functional résumé. They may ask you to draw up a chronological listing or fill out an application blank with the stock questions after they've seen your functional résumé. But realize that it was the functional résumé which got you inside—and that's the first big phase of the battle won.

Employment agents, recruiters and personnel search experts do not agree in their opinions about the functional résumé. Of the relatively few who oppose it, most of them disapprove for reasons of their own profit-making convenience rather than for reasons concerning your best interests.

When you submit a functional résumé to a professional job hunter, you assign him to find you a particular job rather than one he picks to suit his purpose. He may tell you he prefers a chronological résumé because it gives him more flexibility in finding a job for you, or he may say that it gives him a chance to spot some things in your background which might qualify you for some other job.

He's right. The chronological résumé does give him more flexibility—flexibility to stick you in any job he happens to have open at the moment. Lots of job hunters get "stuck" just this way and eventually wind up where they started, looking for another job.

This is highly unlikely to happen to you if you take a little extra time to prepare a good functional résumé.

CHAPTER X

How to Compose a
Result-Getting Résumé

**Determining the job title. Specifying the job functions.
Describing what you have done. Discussing your
personal background.**

This chapter is a step-by-step guide to composing a functional résumé. If you feel that a chronological résumé is sufficient for your needs, turn to pages 89–90 for some helpful suggestions on how to describe your experience most effectively. Then refer to Chapter XVII for a sample modified chronological résumé.

But, if you've decided on a full-fledged functional résumé, begin with the basic understanding that when you write a functional résumé you are not offering the whole hog. You are slicing, trimming, and packaging the edible parts for a predetermined market.

The so-called functional résumé is actually not a résumé at all. That is, it is not a summary of all your past experience. Instead, it is a written proposal of your intentions to proceed to a specified job.

When you compose a functional résumé, you are claiming that you're qualified to perform in a particular capacity. You are basing your claim on certain factual evidence taken from your previous accomplishments.

Begin your functional résumé with an outline. Complete the outline before you attempt to write anything else. Start with the title of the job you propose to perform now, and continue with sub-headings which describe the main activities or functions of that job.

Follow this format:

> Name
> Address
> Phone Number

JOB TITLE

First Function: The most important activity expected of someone performing in the specified job title, i.e., the most essential function from the point of view of the employer's needs.

Second Function: The second most important function of the job according to the employer's needs.

Third Function: The third most important function of the job according to the employer's needs.

Fourth Function: The fourth most important function of the job according to the employer's needs.

Fifth Function: The fifth, and possibly, sixth, function if there actually are that many consequential functions according to the employer's principal needs.

Education (or background)

Personal

As a simple illustration, here is what might be the completed résumé outline of a housekeeper whom we'll call Hattie Handy. Of course, someone in the occupation of housekeeper wouldn't ordinarily have any reason to work out a résumé, but the familiar activities of her job serve as an obvious example of what is meant by "functions." Examine this outline carefully as a model for yours.

Hattie's experience has been gained through several various jobs with intervening periods of unemployment. She was a helper in a busy young family with six small children. She served as ladies room attendant in a private office employing twenty-three young women. Her top-level job was as housekeeper in a plush suburban home with four children, a dog, and a socially active wife.

Now, Hattie wants a very different sort of position with higher pay and less confusion. From her research, she determines a bachelor apartment to be her target. She arranges an orderly résumé outline looking forward to the needs of her next employer.

Mrs. Hattie Handy
123 Warburton Ave.
Yonkers, N.Y. 10701
914-963-5088

Housekeeper—Bachelor Apartment

1. Planning and Cooking Meals

2. Budgeting and Shopping (Food and Light Housewares)

3. Washing and Ironing

4. Light House-Cleaning

Education

Personal

This is the outline of Hattie's proposal. You can see immediately from the specified job title that the applicant knows what she wants to do now regardless of the various directions which her career may have taken her in the past. You can also see just from the carefully selected functional headings that Hattie knows the job and is probably quite capable of performing it. These are two features which will command attention and place any résumé on top of the pile for early consideration.

Completing the résumé is a relatively easy matter of filling in the blank spaces under each heading. Hours of writing and rewriting are saved by planning the outline first.

No matter how advanced you are or how complicated your

line of work may be, your résumé outline can be just as simple and forthright as Hattie's. In fact, the simpler you can make it the more organized and capable you will appear to the employer. Start on your outline now.

Determining the Job Title

The first step in composing a functional résumé is to find the proper job title for the work which you have in mind. This is where research comes into the picture as it does over again throughout your job-finding campaign. Don't guess. Get facts about job titles.

Do not make up a title of your own so that you can conveniently fit your experience into it. If you try to do this, you may be creating an imaginary job and your whole campaign could be fruitless. And do not conclude that other organizations are set up just like your last place of employment with the same job title for the same job. The framework of certain businesses and organizations can be so unique that their job titles, departments, and work-a-day language are entirely different from the average. These are the exception rather than the rule. If your past experience has been with the exception, you could be talking a language which won't make your prospective employer feel at home with you.

Be careful of this detail in everything you write and say, especially if you are making a decided change in the kind of employer you want to work for now. For example, in government and military circles there is a function known as "Procurement." But in the commercial world, the same thing is called "Purchasing." Use the nomenclature of your prospective employer and not your previous employers.

As you investigate your prospects, be aware that even when the organizational set-up of employers is virtually the same, there can be variances in job titles. One employer may have a job called "Director of Public Relations." The next employer thinks of that same position as "Public Information Officer." Still another employer might have a pet name for it like "Manager of Public Affairs." While other employers might be so vague as to identify the job no more specifically than "Assistant to the President."

Obviously, in this case, the most frequently used designation is "Public Relations." And that is the proper terminology for a résumé job title. Sometimes in other fields the difference in nomenclature is not so obvious. Just make certain that you use the terms which are generally accepted in your industry rather than some other language which might happen to be more familiar to you and your past employers.

There are three sources which you can check to be sure you have the right title. They are easily accessible and it takes only a few minutes to find the information you need. Use two of the three following.

Help-Wanted Ads: Glance through any good-sized Sunday newspaper which has a large Help Wanted and Business Opportunities Section. You'll find that the most common nomenclature for the job you're after is repeated almost exactly from one listing to the next.

Directories: Scan the pages of any directory in your field which indicates department heads by name and by title or which specifies organizational detail. Again, you'll find the most common job title terminology repeated. Even if you're not looking for a job as a department head, the title of the man in that position is your key to the language used by associates, assistants, and department workers.

Direct Inquiry: If you're within reasonable distance, you can telephone several of the organizations which you are considering and get this information without identifying yourself. Ask the switchboard operator or receptionist what they call the person in the job which you have in mind. There's nothing secret about job titles. Ask and you'll get the answer.

Finally, do not try to save yourself time by using a title which is so broad that it actually describes two or three jobs. You

don't want several jobs. You want one. The fastest way to get it
is to apply for one job, at least one at a time. This is also the
fastest way to write a good résumé.

Many job hunters think that a job title which covers everything is the easy way out. It isn't, and if you try to use a cover
all title, you'll get into trouble when it comes to writing the
résumé. You'll find you will sound like two different people.

If there are two somewhat different jobs which you feel would
be equally satisfying to you, write two résumés and slant each
one accordingly.

Whatever your particular situation may be, commit yourself
to one job in every résumé you write and specify that job as
definitely as possible in your title. Don't just say "Salesman" or
"Salesman—Intangibles." Say "Insurance Salesman," if insurance
is your proposed direction now. Don't just say "Editor." Say
"Book Editor—Juveniles," if the juvenile books field is where you
are headed. Don't just say "Marketing Executive" say "Resident
Marketing Manager, International," if that's the "office" you're
running for.

Follow the above general rules and that's as far as you need
go in determining your job title. There are volumes of books and
other printed materials on job titles and job specifications. But
these publications are primarily for professional personnel people.
Don't while away your time studying them and involving yourself in hair-splitting technicalities.

Keep in mind that the job title is the subject of your proposal
and the most distinguishing feature of your résumé, even more
important to your prospects than your name. If you use a title
which is fundamentally wrong, you can give the impression that
you aren't really acquainted with the field. If you use a proper
title, you have an excellent start in persuading your prospects
that you know what you are talking about.

It shouldn't take you long to find the right title. If you seem to
be deliberating over this important detail at any great length,
it is either because you haven't made a realistic decision about

what you want to do or because you haven't carried out sufficient research to find the facts you need to know with regard to where you're going.

In the first steps of your job campaign, it has been necessary to analyze your needs and your wants. You have already made definite decisions about these things.

Specifying the Job Functions

Now comes the time to do an about-face, reverse your perspective to the employer's point of view. In specifying the proper functional headings for your résumé, it's a good idea to forget yourself temporarily and concentrate on the employer's predicament.

Most people automatically think first of themselves. They look back over the work they have done and the jobs they have held in sequence. It takes a forward look to organize the functional headings for an effective résumé, and it calls for practice at first. The best way to get that practice is to pick out a single prospect whom you can name and sketch the first draft of your résumé to fit his needs alone.

After you've had practice determining functional headings for one specified employer, you can easily expand your functions to suit other employers, if indeed, that becomes necessary. It might possibly be advisable to change the order of your functional headings slightly from one prospect to another so as to alter the emphasis in different cases. But, generally speaking, if you have a realistic concept of what the job is, there will be no need to make many changes.

In addition, if you practice by specifying functional headings for one employer who actually exists, you are sure to avoid that serious hazard of writing a résumé for one of those imaginary jobs. So write the first draft of your résumé for one single employer. Select one you know something about. Visualize him, the office he works in, his secretary, his assistants, and his organizational set-up. Make it real. Ask yourself, "If I were that employer, what would I want someone in the specified job to do for me starting next Monday morning at nine o'clock?" "Where would he fit into my organization?" "What are the principal four or five activities I would want him to perform?" Those activities are the functions of your résumé. Just place them in the order of their importance to the employer and you'll be sure to get his attention.

From your research you already have a pretty good idea of what he will expect from you. If you have any doubts about it, this is a good time to seek out one final research interview with some employer or friend who can advise you as to the functions of the job.

Then take out your scratch pad and spend an hour working out your résumé outline. Begin by listing in your own language any and all activities which you think you could perform to benefit your selected practice prospect. Jot them down quickly as they come to mind. Do not just think about this list. Write it. Then, put your pencil down and read what you have written aloud to yourself.

Your next move is a simple one of editing to check the following six features:

First, You may find that you've repeated yourself and said what amounts to the same thing in somewhat different language. Eliminate this duplication. While you're rewriting try to use words which indicate action. The easiest way to do this is to start your headings with gerunds like *supervising, coordinating, planning, creating, managing,* or whatever verbs apply to your particular work.

Second, Check each of the remaining activities on your list to decide whether or not it is really applicable to the job specified in your title. If not, cross it off no matter what other feelings you may have about it. Don't hem and haw about this or try to rationalize or justify the inclusion of pet achievements which don't apply directly to the job.

You probably have certain favorite accomplishments which are not applicable to your next employer's needs. And, like most uninitiated résumé writers, you may have inadvertently noted them in your first random list of activities. This is the time to discipline yourself and eliminate what is extraneous from the employer's point of view. Remove this sort of thing in a few minutes now and you'll save hours of struggling to edit it out when you come to writing the résumé. What's more, you'll train yourself to the good habit of considering the employer's position first in everything you write or say in your job campaign.

Third, Go through your list to weed out relatively inconsequential functions so that your résumé isn't going to be padded with matters which actually aren't of much importance to your prospects. The best way to determine this is to ask yourself with respect to each functional heading, "Is this a part of my experience which is going to have any real bearing on the employer's decision about whether or not he's going to interview me?" A good many résumés which are very convincing in the first two or three functions resolve into a disappointing anticlimax toward the end simply because the author didn't know when to stop writing.

Fourth, Check your list again to determine whether or not you have included some activities which, although applicable and fairly important, could be better included under one of your other headings rather than being left to stand alone.

Fifth, When you have completed your cutting job and reduced the list to a hard core of several key functions, you may find that you can combine some of them under one heading. Here is another place where you'll find it to your decided advantage to keep your eye on your prospect. Some activities which you may think of as being separate items, because that's the way they were in the course of your experience, may not be separate items as far as your prospective employer is concerned. For instance, supposing your field were manufacturing and you were seeking a new job as plant manager for a very small manufacturer. Probably one area of activity which you would supervise on your job would be Purchasing. At one time in the past, you had some experience in purchasing raw materials. And at another time for another employer you were involved in purchasing sub-assembly parts. You would naturally think of these activities as two different functions. But the small manufacturer whom you want to work for has one department to serve both these functions. In such a case, you would simply combine into a single heading the two functions which you listed separately in your rough outline. Purchasing Raw Materials and Purchasing Sub-Assembly Parts might become simply Purchasing.

By the same token, your new position might call for a knowledge of fabrication and of finishing. You may have gained your experience in these two areas separately, but the small plant you're going to manage now is organized to handle them as one; so your proper functional heading would be Fabrication & Finishing.

Whatever your field may be, reduce your list of functional headings to the lowest common denominator and adjust them to your next employer's organizational setup. When you do this, your résumé immediately appears like a mirror to your prospective employer and he can quickly visualize himself and you in the same frame. This, of course, is what gets interviews!

Sixth, The last detail in editing your outline is arranging the finished functional headings in the order of their importance to your prospect. Remember to forget your chronology and think of the employer's needs. And keep in mind that you are making a proposal, establishing a claim.

There you have the six key points to guide you in selecting and arranging functional headings for the strongest possible résumé you can write.

These features are the rules. There are some exceptions to the rules, but the exceptions do not apply to you unless you are in an extremely rare situation—and that is very doubtful. So don't prematurely conclude that these rules can't be applied to you.

It is possible that if you are headed toward a new job which represents a radical change in the kind of work that you're going to do from here on, you may have to face the reality that the function which is most important to the employer is one in which your background is weak. If this is the case, you have to make a sacrifice and list that function second or possibly even third so as to get your strongest points across in the first functions. Just make sure that those first functions do have some significant bearing on the job specified in your title.

If the most important function from the employer's point of view is an area in which you have very little or no experience at all, do not try to fake or pad a function. Leave it out entirely.

Should you find yourself in such a predicament, we assume that you're going into this with your eyes open, and that you have decided you have so much excellent experience in the other functions it will offset your weakness in the one. This is possible. However, you'd kill your proposal if you were to mention your weakness in the résumé. Save any discussion of this loophole for the interview, where you have a much better opportunity to get your point across.

Describing What You Have Done

With your job title and functional headings organized, you are well prepared to complete a good résumé. If you wish, you may lead into your résumé with a general opening statement or "scope sentence." At the end of your résumé, you may want to list a few short items about your education and personal status. But, for the time being, stick to the meat of your proposal— your work.

You have established your functional headings as the claims in your résumé. Your next move is to back up each one of these claims with supporting evidence in the form of a simple narrative describing the best of your experience.

The principal content of your narrative under each function should be a detailed example or two of you in action doing what the functional heading describes. You may want to add a very brief sentence at the beginning or end of the examples to show that you've had still more experience in that same category. But the specific examples are the best possible testimony of your ability. They are the hard core of your supporting evidence. So write them first. If you do a good job of describing them, you may find they speak for themselves so that nothing more need be said.

Review your whole background from the beginning to select the examples best suited to the job you're after now. It is possible that a certain phase of your experience acquired several years back can make a better example than your most recent work.

In the interest of keeping your résumé brief and to the point, understand that if in one example you prove you can lift fifty pounds, it is not necessary to use a second example showing that you can lift twenty-five pounds. For example, if a fund raiser relates one top-level instance when he supervised a campaign which raised five hundred thousand dollars for a hospital in Des Moines, it is not necessary for him to enlarge upon another instance when he raised four hundred thousand dollars for a hospital in St. Louis—unless the latter situation called for an entirely different kind of know-how.

Remember that your résumé is just a door-opener to an interview. Samples of your top-level experience will get you the best interviews. The employer knows without your telling him that you have advanced from some lower position. Explanation of your lesser achievements and the admirable progress you have made along the way won't add anything to the persuasivness of your résumé.

Base your selection of examples upon two considerations.

First, which one or two represent the greatest breadth and depth? In other words, which ones will best illustrate "how much you have done" and "how far into" a given area you have penetrated?

Second, which examples come closest to the kind of experience your next employer can use most profitably? In other words, which samples of you at your best will prospects recognize are the sort of problems they are faced with month-to-month, day-to-day? For instance, supposing our fund raiser has had some excellent experience in raising money for schools, churches, and hospitals. Then he applies for a job with a fund raising agency whose principal business is raising money for hospitals. Certainly, the part of the applicant's experience which is of special interest to his prospect is the hospital experience. In fact, that could be the only interest to this prospect. In this case, our applicant might possibly add a very brief scope sentence specifying success in his school and church work. But if he were to elaborate beyond this he would weaken the impact of his strong hospital experience.

Of course, in selecting the best examples, you will find some instances where the illustrations which show your greatest depth and breadth are not the ones which come closest to your prospect's needs. As in the case of working out your functional headings, you may have to make some compromises. Just realize that if you have to make too many compromises of this sort, your job campaign may be going in the wrong direction. Check your research to make sure you're on the right track.

There is a sure-fire prescription for writing up your examples to illustrate you at your best. First, indicate the problem which you faced. Second, describe how you solved that problem. Third, specify what resulted from your efforts. *Problem, Solution, Results.*

These are the A B C's in "experience reporting." They are the essential ingredients which will demonstrate your maximum value to a prospective employer. Keep them in mind every time you write or talk about your experience.

There are two reasons for indicating the problem. The first, as we have already suggested, is to show your prospect that you have been in situations somewhat comparable to those which confront him and his organization. The second reason is that the problem alone sometimes conveys the full meaning of the story.

Were you to tell somebody that one February day, you drove from New York to Boston in six hours, you wouldn't distinguish yourself at all because most drivers can make the trip in that time or less. But, if you began your story by indicating the problem you faced at the time, you would communicate the real significance of that experience, as follows;

"In a blinding February storm of snow and sleet, I drove from New York to Boston in six hours."

This same situation holds true in writing about your work experience. The problem can alter the significance of the whole story. Never assume that your audience understands it was snowing and sleeting no matter how common that may be for the month of February. And never take for granted that because your prospective employers are familiar with the field, they understand the particular conditions you're referring to.

The reason for detailing how you worked out the problem is to give the employer some insight into your way of doing things. More than that, it provides you with an excellent opportunity to show your hand at work and distinguish yourself from the crowd.

When you described that trip from New York to Boston, if you explained that you had carefully studied the weather map twenty-four hours in advance to determine the least congested route, you would show foresight and planning ability which would not otherwise be recognized. Then, if you further stated how you found ways and means to avoid steep hills and get out of rough spots, you would show initiative which your prospects wouldn't have realized. This would set you apart from the average driver. These are the kinds of things which will get you to that interview ahead of the others.

The results are paramount. They are the proof positive of your ability to produce. There might be a few situations when you don't need to elaborate on the problem or the solution. But there is seldom an instance when you can afford to leave out the results expressed in precise terms.

The fact that you drove from New York to Boston would be

relatively meaningless if you did not specify that you arrived safely and delivered the goods on time.

Here are some samples to familiarize you with the problem, solution, results pattern as applied to job function examples. They are samples of three function narratives taken from the successful résumé of a design artist with two years' experience, a public relations man with ten years' experience and a construction engineer with twenty years' experience. These examples represent three entirely different fields and levels, yet all of them follow the same format, indicating the problem, describing the solution, and, finally, specifying the results.

Whatever your field or level of experience, read these samples as a practice exercise to prepare you for writing your own.

A Young Woman Artist With Two Years, Experience

Job Title   *Artist and Designer*

Function   *Designing Three-Dimensional Props and Flat Pieces*

Problem   In my two years out of college, while employed as an Art Dept. Secretary for *Family Circle* magazine, I have worked in my spare time to create display props and flat pieces. Competing against established studios with extensive facilities, I have home-made 10 designs and lay-outs used by a manufacturer, an advertising agency, and a department store.

Solution   I have used advertised products and constructed displays out of aluminum foil, shelf paper, stationery supplies, contact tape, paper plates, cups, doilies, straws, spools of thread, brand name fabrics, plastic refrigerator dishes, wallpaper and candy.

Results   On one project, I made an animal which I called a "Dog-Gone-It" out of an aluminum pan and other aluminum products. My "Dog-Gone-It" was used by a manufacturer on a dozen network television commercials. On request of the manufacturer, I designed a single fold mail piece with simple copy and my Brownie camera photograph of "Dog Gone It." This was circulated nationally exactly as I designed it.

          In another instance, some multi-colored fabric decorations I designed were used by a leading department store

which wrote me, ". . . Congratulations. We had sellouts of
the featured colors."

Woman's Day magazine ran an illustrated article which
included another of my designs featuring brand name
materials An executive of the Eagle Thread Company
said that my design and display was . . . "one of the finest
stimulants to hand knitting to come down the pike in quite
a while."

Notice how, in stating the problem, this applicant used facts
which unquestionably imply initiative, perseverance, enthusiasm,
the ability to work against odds and a personal conviction as to
what she wants to do. These are the qualities which employers
seek in young people. This function description leaves no doubt
that the applicant has them. The originality and inventiveness
which the author displays in her solution show a unique hand
at work, separating her from the mob of aspiring designers.

Obviously, at this point in her career, this young job hunter's
experience wasn't extensive enough to cite impressive amounts
and quantities by number in her results. But observe how her
examples use quotes and name "Macy's", "The Eagle Thread
Company" and "The Young Homemaker's Magazine" to lend a
measure of real authority to the results.

Whether you are a young job hunter or an old-timer, *you* have
worked under difficult circumstances. You have employed your
inventiveness to resolve problems and achieve measurable results.
Tell your prospective employers about them in this manner—
problem, solution, results.

A Public Relations Man With Ten Years' Experience

Job Title   *Director of Public Relations*

Function   *Working With the Press*

Problem   For example, I served as spokesman for the United Broadcasters Association, through two years of an anti-trust suit
against this 20 station combine and as many law firms representing the interests of each station. The suit was launched
when Washington investigations were making headlines
unfavorable to the broadcasting industry as a whole. Our

U.B.A. suit was a conspicuous first of its particular kind and involved some target name personalities.

Solution   To establish a favorable press, I arranged "free lunch" press conferences in the areas of my employers' operations and, in each case, persuaded a popular local figure to act as moderator. In addition, I personally visited each of the wire services and every large city daily paper in the areas of concern to familiarize them with our side of the picture and to plant favorable stories.

Results   Ninety per cent of these papers ran this favorable material and three of my stories received page one placement in papers like the *Chicago Tribune* and the *St. Louis Post Dispatch*. Six of the papers which published this favorable story line were publications which had originally employed back-stairway inquiry techniques to obtain material which would have been detrimental to my employers. Through my two years on the receiving end of hundreds of press probes, less than two dozen consequential stories appeared against the association and all but one were buried in the papers' back pages.

Review this story again. You can readily see how indicating the problem magnifies the importance of the solution and results. In the statement of the problem, notice how well this résumé writer has described one that would challenge any press relations expert. See how much the author has said in some of his very short phrases and sentences "... conflicting interests of each station (and law firms) ...," and "... (other) Washington investigations (of the same industry) ... were making (unfavorable) headlines," and "Our ... suit was a conspicuous first of its particular kind and involved some target name personalities."

In the solution, you can readily visualize the applicant's individual touch at work in his "free lunch press conferences." Beyond any question his statement of facts without personal opinion clearly demonstrates the initiative, organizational ability and drive essential to the job at stake. The numbers and names in the results are the final proof of the man's qualifications.

An interesting sidelight to this story is that the outcome of the trial was a decision against the United Broadcasters Association and every one of its individual members. However, the important feature for the purpose of this man's résumé is the fact that he performed his part of the job very well and achieved excellent results on his particular assignment.

You may have been a part of some activity which was a failure. Nevertheless, if you can show good results in your particular role, you have a good example to use for your function narration.

A Construction Engineer With Twenty Years' Experience

Job Title   *Manager of Construction and Engineering*

Function   *Coordinating Home Office and Sub-contractors*

I have twenty years' experience in the employ of three major construction companies, for whom I have supervised construction of ten industrial facilities ranging in size from a $600,000 plant to a complex $20,000,000 project.

For example, on one assignment I was sent to Canada as my firm's sole representative to build a plant on a tight schedule in time for a client, a chemical company, to fulfill a commitment. I solicited bids, negotiated contracts, and supervised the construction. The start of the project involved some delicate client relations concerning our understanding of the planned capacity. I resolved our differences agreeably and effected changes which increased the plant's capacity 15%. When a jurisdictional union dispute threatened to tie up the job, I arranged talks with national leaders of unions concerned and obtained an agreement which averted work stoppage.

The plant was ready for start up two months ahead of schedule.

On another out-of-town project, to keep within a restrictive budget I gained authorization to negotiate sub-contracts and change orders. My changes and dealings with local contractors made it possible to hold costs of this 150,000-square-foot, steel construction multi-level garage under $11.00 per square foot. Extra work charges were under ¾ of 1% and the profit margin for my employer was about 15%.

Here is a higher-level job hunter using essentially the same format, but with the problems, solutions, and results intermixed. Can you spot them?

At higher levels, indication of amounts and quantities in numbers and figures will convey a lot about your ability, but your prospect still wants to see your hand at work dealing with the kind of problem which he has. It is your description of how you did things which makes the big figures believable. If you are applying for a high-level position, you must make some pretty strong claims. Sometimes the big claims, truthful though they may be, appear unbelievable to your prospects. Hardly ever does a well-established organization want to hire an ingenious lone wolf who claims a string of remarkable single-handed feats.

If you truthfully claimed that you saved your company two million dollars in one year, your prospect might cast your résumé aside because ordinarily no one man can do that without a whole lot of help. But, if you write your solution to demonstrate "supervising," "coordinating," "persuading" and "working with others" to achieve such a result, your strong claim becomes credible and you get an interview.

Of course, if you are applying for a high executive, managerial position, you will be hired in large part for your ability to make harmony out of chaos and to reduce complex activities to the simplest possible form. To suggest this ability, your résumé must reduce to the simplest possible form your own long and complicated experience. Many highly experienced job applicants make the mistake of writing on and on about all the things they've ever accomplished. They wind up with a résumé which looks like a long obituary and usually is as far as their careers are concerned.

Keep it short. The use of facts, figures and a few examples of your hand at work will do the trick for you.

Use these samples as a guide to write your examples. Write the examples for one function at a time. You don't have to start with your first function. Pick the one which seems easiest to you.

The practice you get with the easy one will make the rest of them come faster.

As you write, be fully aware that you are explaining something to a person who knows absolutely nothing about your work. And you want to be sure he understands the full meaning of what you're describing. Make your descriptions as lengthy as you like at first but keep them specific and factual.

After you have written your examples for one function, decide whether or not you need to introduce these with a lead-in sentence which summarizes your additional experience in that category.

When your examples show the breadth and depth of your experience in a given area, you probably won't add anything to your story with an extra sentence which says that you've done the same thing on other occasions, in other places, and for other employers. If you look back to the function sample of the public relations man on page 108, you will see that the applicant doesn't use an introductory scope sentence because the one example he selected represents the best from all his press-relations experience. It speaks for itself without anything further.

However, if you want to show years of experience or some other quantitative measure not indicated in the example, or if you'd like to mention circumstances different from those in the example, or point out several good name employers not in the example, you might add to your story a brief scope sentence. Just make sure that you are saying something which will have an additional influence on your prospective employer.

The following are scope sentences taken from job-winning résumés. Don't make your sentences any longer than these.

Field   *PUBLICITY*

Function   *Writing Newspaper Features*

Scope
Sentence   For the Arno Public Relations Agency, and for Dayton
              & Wells, Inc., I planned and wrote over a thousand jewelry
              fashion features with photos.

One Sunday supplement feature which I prepared ... (specific example)

Field	*ENGINEERING—MARKET RESEARCH*
Function	*Monitoring Electronic Equipment*
Scope Sentence	Over a period of twenty years for Sampson & Co. and for Lloyd-Smith, I have monitored technical developments and marketing problems in electronic equipment. For instance, on one assignment ... (example)

Field	*MAGAZINE SPACE SALES*
Function	*Selling Special Audience Publications*
Scope Sentence	As Eastern Advertising Representative for Jordan Publications for six years, I sold their farm papers to farm occupational accounts such as chemical and petroleum products, drugs and foods, equipment, building materials, and insurance. For example, ... In another instance, ... (second example)

Field	*PURCHASING*
Function	*Researching Commodities*
Scope Sentence	As assistant Director of Purchasing for Levitt Chemical and later for Amalgamated Chemical, I have prepared some fifty economic surveys on organic and inorganic chemicals. For example, ... (specific example)

If you want to change the pace of your résumé, begin your narration under functions, getting directly to the samples. Then, after the specific examples, add your scope sentence, writing something like this.

Function	*Researching Commodities*
	For example, ... (specific example) In another instance, ... (second specific example) ... My experience in this function includes work on similar surveys which I conducted as a member of the purchasing staff for DuPont.

When the narrative for all the functions is completed, review your résumé. Glance over the function headings and read the first few lines under each. Decide then whether you need to introduce the whole résumé with a general opening statement immediately after your job title at the top of the first page.

There is a difference of opinion among our Job Finding Forum people with respect to this detail. Those who advocate a summary opening statement believe that it is a strong attention getter which makes it possible for the employer to understand at a glance just what it is you do and what your level of experience is. The vast majority of employers want to get the gist of what you're talking about quickly. To this end, a well-written opening statement can be a feature which will make your résumé one of the first to be considered.

Other Forumites who oppose opening statements feel that the employer can see nearly the same thing by scanning the functional headings and the first sentence under each. More importantly, if the opening sentence fails to pin-point what he needs, he might not read any further.

Perhaps the answer to this question lies in your research. If you know in advance just what your prospect needs, and can sum up these needs in an opening sentence about your experience, that statement is an obvious attention getter.

Of course, if you are attempting to rise from assistant manager to manager, you might not be able to show managerial status in an opening statement. Or if you are making a major job switch, it's possible that you will not be able to specify experience in the exact capacity you seek now. In such cases you are probably better off to forget a general opening statement and start right off with Function No. 1.

If you do decide to write an opening sentence or paragraph, do not designate it as "Job Objective" or "Position Desired." In a functional résumé, you are not talking about your objectives; you're talking about the employer's objectives. And you're not talking about a position you desire. You're talking about a service you have to offer. The strong selling point of a functional résumé is that you are talking about the employer and his needs. The opening statement needs no title. Place it alone at the top of the page and it will speak for itself.

For examples of good opening sentences, look through the sample résumés in the Appendix. Some of these successful résumés used opening statements. Others did not. Look at both and decide for yourself which is best for your particular circumstances.

If you do write an opening statement, be careful not to cover too much ground. Remember, you can very easily spread yourself too thin and inadvertently create the impression that you're all over the lot.

Now that you have determined the proper job title, worked out your functional headings and written short descriptions to support them, review the following list.

Ten Ways to Polish a Résumé

1. Stick to the facts.

2. Specify amount & quantities by number.

3. Use quotes for emergency only.

4. Name names.

5. Indicate "years."

6. Say "I."

7. Beware the five most misused résumé words.

8. Distinguish yourself.

9. Make your statements worth the money you're asking for.

10. Make it short and neat.

1. STICK TO THE FACTS

You will be free to inject your opinion later in your interviews and phone calls and in a covering letter which you can write to accompany your résumé. But it is essential to state facts and only facts in the résumé.

Don't just talk about your achievements. Demonstrate them. For example, if you want to express the idea that you are tactful, considerate, and get along well with people, do not say "I have always practiced fair play, am tactful and considerate of those who work with me and under me." That's opinion. It's not a statement of fact.

Prove your point this way. "When I was assigned office manager for the Ajax Company, I revamped office procedures to improve working conditions for a staff of thirty clerks confined in crowded space and often working under pressure of deadlines. Over a period of three years under my supervision, personnel turnover was reduced 25 per cent and absenteeism became negligible. This was accomplished without any upgrading of previously established salary scales."

You can see from this factual report that the applicant surely must be fair, tactful, and considerate. He must be able to work very well with people. His point is unquestionably proven by a statement of facts without any expressed personal opinion at all.

2. SPECIFY AMOUNTS AND QUANTITIES BY NUMBER

Make an effort to be definite and specific in every line of your résumé.

Don't say, "For many years, I ..." Say, "For ten years, I ..." Don't say, "I supervised the staff ..." Say, "I supervised a twelve-man staff." Don't say, "I worked on several projects." Say, "... seven projects." Don't say, "Sales reached a new high." Say, "a new high of four million dollars." Don't say, "New business increased." Say, "New business increased 21 per cent."

Specify by the number, but don't crowd too many numbers too close together so that they become confusing. Don't say, "My (work) saved one thousand man hours and five thousand dollars in two months while production increased 15 per cent and deliveries were made ten days ahead of previous schedules."

Be selective instead and use two or three figures at the most, which convey the greatest meaning to your prospects. If you do not know what the amounts and quantities are by the number, go back to your research and get them. If all else fails, say "approximately" and make an honest guess. Some employers will use your résumé in the interview. They will ask about some of the specifics which you mention. So if you are "approximating" or "honest guessing" be able to substantiate it in the interview.

3. USE QUOTES FOR EMERGENCY ONLY

Only when you can't show specific tangible results, use quotes.

You may quote a written statement exactly as it was or a spoken statement as you honestly remember it. Select the highest possible authority which you can find. Also, it's perfectly reasonable to ask one of your past employers to write or say something specific about the work you did for his organization. Quote your achievement. Leave out personal compliments about what a "nice person" you are.

Don't use two quotes in succession. Separate them. Two or three quotes is all you can afford. If you include more than this number, you imply that you can't speak for yourself.

4. NAME NAMES

Associate yourself with good names. This does not mean you should name all your employers or all your associates or, perhaps, all your credits.

Three or four good names of selected employers is about all you need in your résumé. The mention of more employers than this can create the impression you've jumped around too much. Maybe you have. But in a functional résumé it isn't necessary to announce it.

Show your hand at work with fellow employees not only at your level but above and below you. When you refer to these people, do not use names unless their names are so extremely well known in your industry that the association is an impressive one. Usually it's best to identify fellow workers by title. Don't say, "I worked with Mr. Rumford Wentworth." Say, "I worked with our plant manager."

If you want to identify yourself with credits, do not itemize a long list. Simply indicate your scope by specifying a number and citing about three outstanding credits as exemplification. For instance, if you are a magazine space salesman, do not say, "I have sold accounts in the chemical field like Stauffer Chemical Co., Union Carbide, Allied Chemical, Tenneco, Pfizer, Merck Co., Olin, and many more." Say, "I have sold twenty-five leading chemical companies such as DuPont. Dow and Allied Chemical."

If public speaking is an important function of your job, don't write a long list of speaking dates. Just indicate the amount by number and follow it with two or three specific illustrations. If your work is in some sort of engineering or technical research and you've contributed importantly to a good number of new developments, simply specify the number and name two or three of your best examples. If you're a television writer, don't list all your shows, just state the number and cite two or three top examples by name.

5. INDICATE "YEARS"

We have seen successful résumés which did not include any mention of years of experience at all. Your experience could be so short or so long that you might have reason to save this detail for interview discussion—if indeed the subject comes up.

Employers like to know from your résumé how many years you've worked—either the total number or the number of years in one or two of the most important functions.

If the length of your experience is commensurate with the level of the job you're after, it is decidedly to your advantage to specify "years." You can do so right in the beginning if you use a general opening statement. Or you can pick one or two spots in your function narrative to mention "years." In any event, do not mention years more than occasionally in your résumé. More frequent reference to years will start your prospect adding them up and you'll appear old as Methuselah.

Remember, never count on "years of experience" alone. As we've suggested before, it isn't how long you've worked that counts, it's how much you accomplished in that time. Some people manage to stay with one employer for a long while without really accomplishing anything of consequence for that employer. Every sizeable organization has a few people who hang on for years without doing much more than getting to work on time and taking up space. It's important for your résumé not to suggest that you belong in this category.

6. SAY "I"

Always speak in the first person to show yourself in action. Don't say, "Five hundred bicycles were sold." Say, "I sold five hundred bicycles." If that isn't quite true, say, "We sold five hundred bicycles." "We" is an excellent word to use here and there because it automatically suggests you're working cooperatively with other people. Just don't add any glorifying adjectives, adverbs, or phrases.

Do not say, "I took complete charge." Simply say, "I took charge." Do not say, "I supervised the entire operation from beginning to end." Say, "I supervised the operation." Then continue to describe in factual terms what you mean by from beginning to end.

It isn't advisable to start the first sentence of every paragraph with "I," but it is easy to bury an "I" in the body of the narrative. If it comes in the first line of a paragraph you can start some sentences with another phrase. Instead of beginning, "I sold five hundred bicycles for the Wheeling Company," lead off by saying, "For the Wheeling Company, I sold five hundred bicycles."

7. BEWARE THE FIVE MOST MISUSED RÉSUMÉ WORDS

"Responsibility"—Do not say, "I was responsible for (something)." The fact that you were responsible for something does not mean that you carried out that responsibility well, if at all. Talk about what you actually did, not what you were supposed to do.

"Duties"—You're not in the army now. Do not say, "My duties were (such and such)." It implies that someone had to stand over you with a big stick to force you to do things. Like responsibilities, the word duties doesn't mean that you actually carried out what you were supposed to do.

"Handled"—Never say, "I handled (such and such)," even if you think your employer knows the field and will understand without further explanation. You mean something more than handled. Exactly what do you mean? That's what your prospects want to know.

"Opportunity"—In a résumé, you're not talking about your opportunity. Instead, you are suggesting between every line that you represent the employer's opportunity to hire a good man.

And don't say, "(Someone) gave me the opportunity to (do such and such)." This implies that you depend on lucky breaks to achieve success. In reality, you probably earned and deserved it. Nobody gave it to you. In any event, you will surely have to earn it on your next job.

"Etc."—Etceteras have no place in your proposal. If what you have in mind is worth your employer's attention, spell it out in detail. If it's not that important and it probably isn't forget it. Don't dribble away your good experience with etceteras. Keep your audience interested.

8. DISTINGUISH YOURSELF

Review each sentence and paragraph, asking yourself, "Does this distinguish me from the average person? Or is what I am talking about just an ordinary, routine procedure?" You can't show that you are a superman in every function of the job, but you probably have a little something special to offer in most instances. What is it? Do your sentences illustrate it?

9. MAKE YOUR STATEMENTS WORTH THE MONEY YOU'RE ASKING FOR

If it's more money you're seeking, check each functional story to see if what you've said is really up to the level of the salary you're asking for. Look out for this one. Your prospects surely will.

10. MAKE IT SHORT AND NEAT

The average good résumé runs two pages or a little shorter. Three pages is the maximum for any résumé. Whatever your background may be, if you go beyond three pages, you'll indicate a lack of organization and direction. No matter how much experience you have, if you write more than three pages, some of what you've written is surely below your top level. Two pages is much better than three. And very often, one page and a half is still better.

The vast majority of employers prefer brevity. They want just enough to give them a clear picture of you, enough to help them decide whether or not they want to see more of you in an interview. Within the maximum limit of three pages, a résumé can be as long as it holds interest. But the employer whose attention can be sustained for three pages is rare. And out of his pile, he's quite likely to read the short ones first.

Read over your résumé and see what you can cut to make it shorter. What have you said that really doesn't add very much to your story? Cut it. What have you said in a long sentence which could be said in a shorter one? Rewrite it. What have you said in two sentences which could be said in one? Combine them. What have you said in a sentence that could be said in a phrase? Shorten it. Think as if you were writing a telegram and paying ten cents a word. Don't waste your dimes or the employer's time with unnecessary words. Make it look short too.

A one page résumé will not look short if you jam the page with solid black type from top to bottom and from side to side. Leave some white space between each heading and between paragraphs. If you want to do an exceptionally good job of it, place the paragraphs so they form a reasonably proportionate pattern with long and short paragraphs alternating. Use the sample résumés in this book as a pattern.

We do not recommend that you have your résumé reproduced in mass because it's better to send out a relatively small number of individually slanted résumés. An individually typed résumé is more personal, more courteous, and above all, suggests your special interest in the employer. The employer knows that you are directing your communication to him and that your résumé isn't just one of a hundred copies which you have dropped in a mail box.

There may be circumstances which would justify reproducing your résumé in quantity. If so, do not make it too fancy or slick so that it looks like a production you've spent a lot of money on. And steer clear of colored ink or paper.

Many of our successful Forum people have adopted a middle of the road policy in reproducing résumés. They have the résumé reproduced in limited quantity by one of several processes which are similar to an individually typed page. If you follow this procedure, use care to match the type of your typewriter and the degree of blackness projected by the ribbon with the résumé. And use the same paper stock and envelopes for your individual covering letters. Résumé reproducing services are inexpensive and easy to find.

Discussing Your Personal Background

If you have a good education, specify it as one last little piece of evidence to support your claim. In the event that you are a young job hunter with little business experience, you may benefit by elaborating slightly on your major subjects and extra-curricular activities, especially if they bear on the job you want now. If you are at a higher job level and have pursued some advanced studies related to your job, it will add a little extra something to describe those studies in a few words.

Do not elaborate on schooling which is completely removed from the job at stake no matter how justifiably proud you may be of your education. You're not looking for prestige. You're looking for a job. If your résumé were titled "Assistant Comptroller'" and you mentioned that you were a graduate of the Juilliard School of Music, you might create the impression that you are indecisive and unsteady.

In any instance, do not write out a long detailed description of your education unless the job you want is of an academic nature and requires certain studies and degrees.

Ordinarily you need only itemize the following specifics in this order: any degree or other certificate you received; the name of the institution or institutions which you attended; any honors or other distinguishing recognition you might have been awarded. Unless the academic institution which you attended is little known, do not indicate its geographic location. Include these details in not more than two or three lines something like this.

Education

    A.B. University of Michigan

or

Education

    Graduate—Rhode Island School of Design
    Advanced Courses in Design—Pratt Institute

or

Education

    A.B. Brown University
    M.A. Cornell
    Ph.D. in Business Administration—Columbia University

or

Education

    A.B. University of Southern California—Phi Beta Kappa

Describe an academic award in terms which your prospective employer will understand. If the award is a nationally known honor like Phi Beta Kappa, indicate it just as is. But if you received an award with a designation peculiar to one academic institution, explain what it was very briefly rather than use the exact title. For instance, if your college awards a citation for journalism called the "Horace Whiteman Award," your prospect won't know what that is. In such case say something like "Honors in Journalism" or perhaps "Special Award in Journalism."

Should you not have completed the full course at a given school or college, do not indicate anything more than the name of the institution. Don't say "Attended" or specify "Two years." Do not defensively explain that you ran off and got married in the middle of your junior year but that you are now repenting by going to night school to get your degree. This may be a big issue in your life but it has little or no meaning to your employer, especially if you are well qualified.

If you jumped from one college or school to the next, limit your list to the one or two institutions in which you took the more advanced work or, perhaps, the one college from which you received a degree. If you have only a high-school education and the job which you are applying for ordinarily calls for a college background, do not mention your education at all unless you have pursued extensive courses in some advanced institutions.

When it comes to describing your personal situation, place it last in your résumé and make it short because personal details are only incidental at this stage.

You might specify your marital and family status if it implies that you are a well-adjusted individual. You can indicate your memberships, if they are in well-known organizations and bear a relationship to the job. You can also mention your community activities, especially if you can show in a short phrase some measure of achievement or standing in them. And you might include three or four words about your military service.

Use your judgment about these details. You may mention any one or all of them so long as you use "telegram" language and don't exceed a total of three typewritten lines. Hold fast to brevity. A lengthy elaboration looks as though you're trying to gild the lily or defend your station in life. Do not simply list the activities which you happen to be proud of. Keep the employer in mind. Make every item count for something from his point of view. Check yourself to make sure that the features which you include are actually conveying to the employer the same thing that they mean to you. If you were chairman of some important committee for three years and the results under your leadership were unusually good, spell out those results in two or three words if the achievement is up to the level of performance described in the résumé.

Should you be applying for a position such as a pay job with the State Democratic Committee or Publicity Director for the Protestant Episcopal National Council, you can add something to your claim by identifying yourself as a Democrat or Episcopalian. But in any other situation, do not indicate any affiliation which will reveal or even suggest your political or religious beliefs. Business is business. Don't confuse it with personal issues. You could be waving a red flag in front of the prospective employer who doesn't share your personal views.

Whether or Not to Mention Age

This is a matter of choice. Your age is a detail that may come out sooner or later, but if you know that your years are not an advantage, it isn't necessary to make an announcement of them in your résumé. Don't be deliberately misleading about this. No matter what kind of original trick you think you have up your sleeve, you can't fool an employer about your age for any consequential length of time, even though he or she is not allowed to ask you directly.

Generally speaking, if your age is very much over or under the bracket considered normal for the job at stake, save mention of it for the interview. If you feel your years present a formidable barrier, this is probably your concern more than the employer's. He probably isn't making as much of an issue over this detail as you are. The way to rid yourself of this mostly imagined obstacle is to concentrate on showing the employer the benefits in store for him if he hires you. Remember, if he wants you badly enough, there are usually ways for him to get around company policies and rules regarding age.

Anyway, if you show a great deal of experience in your résumé, your prospective employers will know perfectly well that you aren't any spring chicken.

On the other hand, if you are quite young but can honestly point to some high-level experience, your prospects may question the credibility of your claims when your résumé announces that you are only twenty-three years old. Even if an employer does accept your job accomplishments as truth, he may decide that "Age 23" in itself alone indicates you don't have the maturity he needs—and you are crossed off his list without further ado.

A statement of your health, good or bad, is entirely unnecessary at this point. If you have some handicap which affects your work seriously and if you judge that in good faith you must advise your prospective employer of this, wait for the interview. By that time, you may decide that there's no need to mention it anyway.

Do not include any statistics of your height and weight. White collar workers are not hired by the pound or linear measure.

It is not advisable to include a list of references at the end of your résumé. When your prospects become interested in you, they will probably ask for references. But they don't need them now. Moreover, practically everybody has good references so that yours are not going to distinguish you or add any persuasiveness to your résumé. In fact, a list of the people who'll vouch for you will only serve to clutter your proposal and make it look long.

The kind and number of references you use will vary from one prospect to the next. Your ready list of them belongs in your job-finding brief case or portfolio.

Now you have all the ingredients to make up the best possible résumé for your needs.

Look over some of the sample résumés in Chapter XVII. See if you can spot the problems, solutions, and results. Then start writing your own.

Important as a résumé is both as a practice instrument and a useful document, you can't afford to spend months writing it, editing it, and rewriting it again. If you find yourself badly confused, your difficulty may be inadequate research. Go back to the source of the trouble.

There is no such thing as a perfect résumé. Do as thorough a job on it as you can, within a reasonable portion of the time you've set aside for your whole campaign. If you have the right job title, the correct functions properly described, and your narrative checks out with the ten points on page 115, you have a good résumé.

Get on to the important business of seeing your prospects.

CHAPTER XI

How to Write a Letter
That Will Get You an Interview

**Four general cautions. The five essential ingredients.
What to do if you have very little or out-dated experience.
Check list for an introductory letter.**

One perfectly good way to establish new contacts is to write a letter introducing yourself.

You should have a good résumé worked out by now. If so, you need only a short covering letter to add a personal, individual touch and to persuade the prospective employer to turn the page and read the résumé.

If you've decided you have either too little, or too out-dated experience to make up an effective, complete résumé, you can get your whole story in a somewhat longer introductory letter.

The primary purpose of an introductory letter is to open the door to your prospective employer's office. Once you are inside, you can sell your qualifications to far greater advantage because when you talk with an employer you can quickly learn a lot more about his interests. Remember, the more you know about him and his organization, the better you can emphasize that part of your background which fits into his particular picture.

So, in the introductory letter, give your prospective employer just a little taste of something which will make him want to *see* you. If you give him too much in the letter, you can kill his appetite prematurely.

When you sit down to write, remember that your prospect has other letters to read beside yours. And to get the attention you want, your job-finding letter must stand out.

Brevity can be your first attention-getter, especially if your competitors for the same job are inclined to be long-winded. Many job hunters seem to feel it's necessary to construct a lengthy preamble about their life situation and elaborate on all the "whys" and "wherefores" before they get to the point. Indeed, there seems to be a natural tendency in a lot of us to want to "explain away" things which may be of consequence to us but which actually mean little to the person we are addressing.

We all have our personal involvements! You don't have to "explain away" yours in a job-finding letter. You don't have to explain why you are leaving or have already left your last job. No matter what the circumstances may be, you do not have to explain in your letter why you are making a job change now.

If you are a man who is a little bit older than you'd like, don't announce it by mentioning "years." If you feel you're too young, disregard this also.

Whatever your situation may be, if you insist on "thinking" there is some loophole in your background which you must defend, this is your problem. Don't make it the employer's problem. Don't call it to his attention and rub it in by trying to explain it in your letter.

If you have a physical handicap which affects your ability to perform your work, do not proclaim it in your introductory letter. Wait for the right time to discuss it. And that right time is after you have proven your many strong points and gained the employer's confidence in you. Then, if you feel it's absolutely necessary in all honesty, you can face the employer with the one thing which you are guessing may be a liability.

In any event, try not to be expansive in your introductory letter. Make it brief—and get it on the paper so that it looks brief.

And you don't need gimmicks to distinguish your letters of application for the same reason you don't need a gimmicked-up résumé. Just tell the employer in straight-forward language that you have certain qualifications and interests which you would like to put to work for that organization.

Don't be oversolicitous. You don't have to plead with your prospective employer to get him to see you. When he decides to set aside some of his supposedly valuable time to confer with you, it is not because he wants to do you a favor. It is because you have given him reason to suspect that you may be of tangible help to him.

Avoid flattery. Employers know how wonderful they are. It doesn't do you any good to tell them you think so too. In fact, your acknowledgement of their distinguished status is not going to persuade them to recognize *yours.* Remember, it is *your* status, *your* qualifications you are selling, not the employer's.

Watch out for exaggerated expressions of gratitude. Be polite, of course. But don't over-extend yourself unnecessarily by saying "I would be very deeply grateful to you for an opportunity . . ." Keep in mind that between the lines you are writing about their opportunity to hire someone with your background. Exaggerating your expressions of gratitude can kill your approach by twisting it so that it appears to be *your* opportunity.

Be careful not to editorialize superfluously. Job hunters are inclined to start their letters with some apropos generalization about the prospect's particular business, or professional, field of concern. Then, these well-meaning letter writers continue with some bit of philosophy about why it would be a good idea for the employer to hire them. This is old hat.

The employer knows the general conditions in his field and sometimes he knows them better than you do. And he's supposed to have his own good reasons for selecting the employees he wants. Whether or not he actually has these good reasons, you run the risk of insulting his intelligence when you expound on why a person in his position should hire an applicant like you.

Give him the facts about your background, experience, and interests and let the facts speak for themselves. Even if you are an experienced professional writer, it is not usually advisable to attempt editorializing because most writers seem to fumble when it comes to writing a job-finding letter for themselves.

So much for the "don'ts" and for general cautions in composing your introductory letter.

Here are the five essential ingredients to write into your letter. Read them slowly. Then, review them thoughtfully. They are what you need, and they are all you need to include in the letter which is going to get you inside.

1. Whenever possible, begin with a brief mention of an appropriate observation regarding either the person you are addressing or the organization he represents. Use any pertinent item so long as it is factual rather than editorial and so long as it establishes your letter as an individual communication rather than as a mass mailing.

2. In a sentence or two, define the scope and depth of your experience. Include "years" of experience or, if you prefer, a definitive measure of them. Mention the name of one *but not more than two* of your employers. Indicate the general line of work you have done and express it in a way which emphasizes that phase of your experience most relevant to the job you are applying for now. You may very logically want to change the emphasis from one prospect to the next.

3. Call attention to your attached résumé and cite one, but not more than two, very abbreviated samples from it. When you shorten your examples for use in the letter, the results and other key statistics are usually the important features to retain. Select the samples most applicable to the job you are seeking. Again you may very logically decide to use different samples for different prospects.

4. Tell your prospect that you want to work for him or her. Make it perfectly clear what work it is that you would do. Specify your job title if possible, but don't guess at it.

5. Ask for an appointment for a person-to-person conference. Always express this important detail so that the follow-up move is yours and in your control. Tell the employer what you want to see him about, but only if this adds some more specific promise that his time with you will be well spent.

Any short introductory letter which contains the above five essential ingredients, and no more, will serve your purpose well. Write this letter in your own language, but look at the following samples first.

In the case of all samples used in this book, most of the personal and company names have been changed. Except for this detail, these letters appear substantially just as they were written by successful job finders.

Don't be concerned if they refer to an occupation which is not yours and if they were written by people with greater or less experience than you. For whatever your work may be, from technical research to commercial art—and regardless of the experience you've had—you should get excellent results from an introductory letter with a format and content similar to these samples. So read them to get the general idea. Re-examine them, point by point. See if you can find the five basic elements in each letter.

Mr. Arthur J. Landing, General Sales Manager
Smith & Reynolds, Inc.
900 Michigan Blvd. S.
Chicago, Ill. 60603

Dear Mr. Landing:

Your speech at the Training Directors convention last January and your recent article in *Sales Management* magazine emphasize a subject of special interest to me, "proper use of visual sales aids."
This is an area in which I have concentrated a great deal of thought and effort in the course of my twelve years with the Ajax Corporation. In more recent years, as an Assistant General Sales Manager here, I have established an intensive program to train our salesmen in proper use of visuals and, perhaps more importantly, to motivate the salesmen to *use* them.
The results are in!

Over a two-year period, the sales of one of our most successful product lines increased 21% above its previously established high. And one of our perennially weak lines moved from near the bottom up to fourth place in the national market in three years' time.

My attached résumé describes how the effective application of visual sales aids figured importantly in these and other substantial Ajax gains. It also briefly outlines other phases of my experience which I would like to put to work for Smith & Reynolds as your sales training director.

Early next week, I will telephone you for an appointment at your convenience to discuss in more detail exactly what I believe I can contribute to your fine sales organization.

Yours truly,

John Madden

400 Raleigh Place
Barrington, Ill. 60010
312–218–3554

1420 Grand Blvd. E.
St. Louis, Mo. 63107
314–621–4320

Mr. John Smith, Executive Director
Paint & Wallpaper Dealers Association
444 Madison Ave.
New York, New York 10016

Dear Mr. Smith:

I am very much interested in the trade-talk speculation that you are considering adding a store-planning service to your association activities.

As director of such a service, I can contribute my ten years experience with the Sure-Sales Fixture Company, St. Louis, for whom I have designed and supervised construction of approximately 100 paint and wallpaper store interiors. This experience includes engineering of special display equipment as well as selecting shelving, counters, color bars and wallpaper tables.

The attached résumé illustrates the increased business which resulted from my work for our clients ranging from smaller stores such as Mates & Garner in Kansas City to larger stores like Harvey's in Baltimore. The résumé further describes how my employer has profited from my trade convention activities and the articles I have written for *Paint and Varnish Production, Coloramic, and Painter and Allied Trade Journal.*

I am quite well acquainted with some of your member firms and the excellent services your organization has provided them, especially over the last three years. I would be proud to be part of it.

I would like to come to New York to suggest a step-by-step plan to put your proposed store-planning service into effect. In a week I will telephone you long distance to learn when a conference will be convenient for you and possibly some of your board members.

Yours truly,

Alvin R. Radner

Mr. George Aiken, President
Giant Advertising Agency
260 Madison Avenue
New York, New York 10016

Dear Mr. Aiken,

I have been informed that your agency has become interested in international advertising and that you have spent considerable time and approximately $200,000 to investigate this market.

I have been managing the International Department for this (4A) agency for almost five years. I am seeking a change.

Please study the enclosed résumé. It demonstrates, I believe, that my knowledge of this field could place you on an operational basis in the international advertising business without further experimentations.

I will call you the first of next week to arrange an appointment.

Please understand this is confidential. I am still employed.

Sincerely,

John DuBois

Roaring Brook Road
Chappaqua, New York 10514
914–218–6314

If you have been able to spot the five basic elements in these letters without too much difficulty, and if you understand them clearly, get to work now on your own letter. You can follow the samples, thought-for-thought, almost paragraph-for-paragraph. Or you can word the letter in your own way. Just make certain that you include all of the five basics, and no more!

Begin your letter. Get yourself off to a good start by making sure the employer's name is spelled correctly and the title is exactly right. Misspelling the employer's name can be like waving a red flag in front of a bull. So is a not-quite-right title. Leave it off if you are not sure of it.

When you finish writing, skip the next pages and turn to the check list on page 148 to make sure you have prepared an introductory letter which is going to get results. If you have questions in your mind about the basic elements or other important details, you will find further explanation of them in the following pages. Simply turn to the heading or headings which concern you.

If you do not have a résumé and are writing a letter which must pave your way to the interview, by itself alone, turn now to page 141.

Composing the Introductory Paragraph

If you still question the urgency of sending out an individual, personalized letter to each prospect, this is a good time to remind you that when employers have very good job openings that have been announced, it is not unusual for them to receive at least fifty letters of reply accompanied by résumés. They then resort to a process of elimination. Often among the first to be dropped are those extra-long, bulky applications, simply because they just don't have the time to pore over them.

The last applications to remain for serious consideration are often those which convey the thought that the job hunter knows something specific about the prospect's organization and the people who run it, and that the applicant has a genuine interest in working for that organization. Hence, a sincere, individualized introductory letter gives you that much more assurance that your letter and résumé are placed very near the top of the pile.

When an employer has not announced a job opening because he's only thinking about it, or perhaps hasn't thought about it at all, your letter must sell him on the idea that it might be worth his while to see you and talk it over.

To accomplish this purpose, it takes a factual, pertinent opening paragraph with specific references like those we have just illustrated. Look at the sample letters again with this in mind.

We have conceded that you do not necessarily have to make up a different résumé for each employer. This is primarily because you get the chance in your individual covering letter to highlight that part of your background which is particularly applicable to each one of your prospects.

Hence the opening paragraph of this letter is the key difference from one application to the next. If you have done your research well, and if you have *real* prospects as we defined them earlier, you won't have much trouble finding an appropriate item for an opening remark.

In fact, if you have any serious difficulty in locating a good item or in fitting it into your story, it might well be a sign that you have shortchanged yourself in one of the most important steps of a successful job-finding campaign, research. However, don't waste your time casting about for an artificial item to open your letter. It can be like looking for a needle in a haystack. What's more, an item which you find in such a hasty manner might sound as though you were stretching a point. Instead, go back to the chapters on research and find out where you overlooked that important something. It's there. And you need it to get the job you want.

Describing the Scope and Depth of Your Experience

By scope and depth, we mean how much experience you have over-all and how far into things you have penetrated.

In defining your scope, it is usually simplest and most effective to specify years of experience—if you have enough of them to substantiate your story well and if their number is logically commensurate with the accomplishment you are showing. If not, or if you have factual reason to again suspect that your too many or too few years may go against you, do not call attention to this by announcing numbers of years anywhere in your letter. Instead, spell out how much experience you've had in other terms like the number of projects you have worked on, the number of dollars involved, or any other number which indicates that you have sufficient amount of experience to fill the job at stake.

In describing depth, do not itemize every major phase of your experience and how far into each phase you have penetrated. Instead, enlarge only on those aspects of your background which are of immediate concern to each employer. Usually these are the one or two parts of your work which tie naturally into your opening remark.

The applicants who wrote the sample letters have experience in depth other than that which they cite, but notice that for purposes of the letter they limit themselves to a single issue of importance to the employer. This is the foot in the door. And this is enough.

You can do the same thing in your introductory letters. Supposing, for example, that you were a plant supervisor with production experience in quality control, fabrication, and finishing. You are applying for a job where you know that one area of special concern to a prospective employer is in quality control. Even if it happens to be a small plant which calls for one man to work all three phases of production, you are well off to limit your first paragraphs in the letter to quality control and go into some depth on that subject alone.

In your last paragraph when you ask the employer for an interview, you could advantageously mention that you would also like to talk to him about your fabrication and finishing experience. But you would spread yourself too thin and weaken your introduction if you threw the whole business at him in the letter.

As another example, suppose that you were a fund raiser with good experience in raising money for hospitals, churches, colleges, and private schools. If you were then to apply for a full-time job as the head of development at Trinity College, your scope and depth sentence might well read, "My fifteen years of fund-raising experience includes organizing and directing successful campaigns for three colleges." Then you could describe one or two of those campaigns. That's sufficient for the letter.

Remember, your primary purpose in the letter is to persuade him politely to read the résumé which gives more information. And when you go to your interview, you can offer still more. But not now, not in your introductory letter.

Selecting the Right Names

It is necessary to mention one or two employer's names which, by association, will help your prospect to identify you favorably. Many job hunters are shy about this at first. They feel that it is advisable to wait for some specific indication of interest on the part of a prospective employer before they spread their present or past employers' names. Applicants feel this way because they are afraid somebody will find out. The fact is that up to the point of final reference, the news that you are looking elsewhere rarely gets back to your present or past employers. And, even if it does, it's just as likely to do you good as harm.

Whatever small chance is left, you must take, for you cannot successfully play hide and seek with prospective employers. If you deliberately omit names from your letters, you are unnecessarily placing your reputation open to suspicion. When you fail to mention a name or two, your prospect automatically thinks, "What's the big secret?", and he puts your application aside to consider one from somebody else who is not so obviously trying to "play it cozy."

A good rule to follow is to use one but not more than two, employer's names in your letter. If you mention more than two employers, their names will overshadow yours. You can't hide behind these names no matter how distinguished they may be. Again remember, it's you whom you are selling, not the people you have worked for.

Ordinarily, it is best to limit your names to organizations and not refer to individuals, unless you know that in a specific instance one name has particular meaning to that prospective employer whom you are addressing. Watch out for this detail. It is commonly overlooked.

"Mr. Sam Summers," Executive Vice President of your present organization, may be a very important man to you, but your prospective employer probably doesn't know Sam. Use the firm name, not Sam's. If you want to pinpoint your reference further, you might use Sam's title but, in most cases, not his name.

In selecting the names which you refer to in your letters, think of your prospective employer and of the significance which the names you mention have for him, not necessarily for you.

For example, you may have had a long association with Smith and Company and a much shorter affiliation with Jones and Company which is less important to *you*. But, if Jones and Company has more good meaning to the man whom you are writing, Jones and Company is the name for you to use in your letter if you can tie it in logically.

Selecting and Abbreviating Examples From Your Resume

You have a résumé. Select one or two examples from it which are applicable to the theme of each letter and to the needs of each employer. You may possibly use the same examples in every letter you write, or you may have reason to vary them according to what is pertinent in each individual letter. Usually the results are the most important feature to retain in the abbreviated form for your letters. But there can very well be certain

job functions where the problem or the solution has more meaning to the employer you are addressing and the particular situation to which you are referring. You know the circumstances
best. Use your own judgment.

Boil the selected examples down to the key points. Don't worry
if it means that parts of some sentences will be repeated in your
letter as they are written in the résumé. If it represents you at
your best, it's *worth* repeating. However, if you use a quotation
from a past employer to substantiate your point, try to limit
yourself to *one* such quote in the letter.

Describing What You Propose to Do Now

It is surprising how many letters of application are written
without asking for the job. The applicant just assumes that the
employer will understand that the author wants a job. As we
have warned before, you must not *assume* anything in your job
campaign, from the first steps to the last detailed matters of
salary and hours. Your introductory letter is no exception.

Make it perfectly clear that you want to work for the employer
and specify, as far as possible, what it is you want to do for
him. When you omit this detail, you imply that you would just
as soon work for anybody in any job. Your letter will have lost
its punch in failing to convey that you are a person who knows
what he wants. Employers need this qualification as much as
anything you can offer them. In many cases, the will to do the
job can be every bit as important as your record of experience.
And the more specific you are about how you can be of help to
your prospective employer, the more convincing you will sound.

Closing With the Next Move in Your Control

End every letter you write so that the next move is up to *you*
and not the employer. Advise him politely that you're going to
telephone, wire, or write to him in follow-up. And tell him when
you propose to do so. This way you keep control.

Say something like "Early next week I will telephone you for an appointment at your convenience" or "Next Tuesday afternoon I will telephone your office to learn when it will be convenient for you to see me." Be positive by saying "when it will be convenient for you to see me," not "when it might be convenient for you to see me."

Maybe you feel that it would be more polite or perhaps easier on your pride if he were to call you. But this is not the time for concern over such delicacies. You can't afford to spend your job-finding days sitting by the telephone or marking time at the mail box awaiting the whims of any one employer. You must keep at every prospect and don't stop until he has committed himself one way or the other. *You* make the advances. Don't wait for *him* very long.

When you apply for a job which is far enough away and calls for consequential travel to the interview, there are a number of ways to arrange a meeting. Advise the employer by letter that you will phone him long distance to set up an appointment. Use the expression "long distance." He may wish to write you before your call; and this may hasten his response. Or notify him that, in a week, you will write him to arrange a personal meeting. This gives him time to study your résumé. It also gives him time to write you a reply first, possibly suggesting that he or his representative will be in your vicinity on certain dates. If he does not reply, the next move is still in your control and you may write a second letter reminding him of your application.

This is one more method to keep your name before him. Every way you can do this counts.

Perhaps you have just finished school or college and are looking for your first full-time job. Maybe you've only had a year or two of regular employment. Possibly, for some good reason, you are starting to work for the first time a little late in life or you are going back to work after years of absence. Maybe you have decided to step in such an entirely different career direction that not very much of your past employment experience applies to the job which you're after now.

In situations like these you will probably do best to write your whole sales story in the introductory letter and not use a résumé. This type of letter must then set forth your interests and qualifications completely. It may be longer than those we have previously discussed but try to limit it to one page. Don't extend a letter of this sort to more than two pages. If you have more than two pages of qualifications to talk about, you probably have enough for a résumé.

Understand that there are lots of good substitutes for job experience. It is actually possible, in some circumstances, to project these substitutes so strongly that they can have more meaning than a record of employment.

A job applicant can be well qualified for a given job on the basis of some of the following: courses and degrees, other special training or schooling, extra-curricular activities, aptitude and vocational interest test results, part-time jobs, travel and other vacation activities, hobbies, volunteer work, social activity, private-life experiences, and many more. Any activity which represents accomplishment or acquired know-how and is directly applicable to the job you want is a good selling point for you.

Many persons, some young, and some not so young, have found their way to highly rewarding new jobs using such qualifications as a foot-in-the-door.

Enterprising young people compose result-getting letters of application by harnessing their studies together with extra-curricular activities, travel, and part-time jobs. Mothers with grown children return to work by capitalizing on some phases of the very realistic, practical experience they learned from running a household and raising children. People with valuable practice in volunteer work, hobbies, and social activities adapt their avocational knowledge to good pay jobs especially when they can show a measurable achievement and tangible benefit to a prospective employer.

Here are four examples of introductory letters written by applicants who did not have enough experience or the right experience to write a résumé. The applicants are different ages with various backgrounds, interests, and personal circumstances. Yet notice that each letter contains very much the same ingredients. Read all four of them so that you can grasp the general pattern which makes these letters effective.

A YOUNG HIGH SCHOOL GRADUATE
SELLS HIMSELF WITH THIS LETTER

Mr. Philip E. Lorn, President
Denton & Rolls, Inc.
347 Madison Ave.
New York, New York 10016
Dear Mr. Lorn:

Your reputation as a resourceful, hard-working agency respected for quality work and service, tells me Denton and Rolls is where I want to work. I like the thoroughness with which you prepare your advertising and your proven ability to get goods sold. You try for the best and I won't be satisfied with anything but the best. That is why I want to work for you.

I am offering you the option on high potential creative ability in return for a copy trainee job as I learn with Denton & Rolls.

Advertising Is My Field: I like moving goods in my mind. I received an "A" rating for the field of advertising in the Strong Vocational Interest Test.

Copy Is My Department: I enjoy getting ideas into writing. My A.A.A.A. examination report says I have "a lively imagination and a facile command of language."

Package Products Are My Accounts: I learned selling in a department store. Now that I know something about the consumers' point of view I can sell better for your clients.

Beyond this basic training, I have nothing to unlearn.

I have developed some ideas which I realize would be of no interest to you except as an indication of my potential value to Denton & Rolls. I would like to show them to you so you can see for yourself the creative ability I am offering you.

I shall call your secretary on Wednesday to arrange an interview at your convenience.

Yours truly,

John Taber

26 Sydney Street
Brooklyn, New York 11205
212–626–1492

Many job-finding letters which were written in more formal business language have wound up in the employer's waste basket. But the President of this large advertising agency took time from his busy schedule to interview this boy and hire him.

Why?

1. Because John Taber is interested and enthusiastic.

2. Because he knows what he wants and where he's going.

3. Because he sets out his qualifications, one, two, three, and is specific in describing them.

4. Because he has taken the initiative to work up some material for demonstration purposes.

5. Because of those five words, "I have nothing to unlearn. This is not a new idea. That sentence has been used by other job finders. But it is still sweet music to a haggard executive who is surrounded from day to day by subordinates and others who think they know more about how to run the business than he does.

Older job applicants would do well to follow this direct, simple, and unsophisticated approach in their letters. Here are a few.

A YOUNG MAN OF FIFTY-TWO GETS HIS FIRST
FULL-TIME JOB WITH THIS LETTER

Mr. Porter Darnborough, General Sales Manager
Seacraft, Inc.
Bayonne, New Jersey 07002

Dear Mr. Darnborough:

I have followed your new advertising approach with a great deal of personal interest.

Last year I bought a new "Seacraft 42," the most serviceable boat I have ever owned. It is my fifth Seacraft in twenty-four years.

Boating has been my life and I have stuck with Seacraft for exactly the same reasons you are advertising now, "Easy handling, dependability, economy."

I should know.

I have fished off the Florida coast in winter, cruised the Chesapeake in spring and sailed Long Island Sound summers—with Seacraft. Between seasons, I have done practically all of my own hull and engine maintenance work and have written several articles which have appeared in *Motor Boating & Sailing* and in *Yachting*.

On many occasions through the years I have participated in Eastern seaboard major-market boat shows as a "temporary" manufacturer's representative.

Now, as an at-large sales representative for you I want to sell your boat.

When I discussed this intention with my old friend and yours, Dick Compton, he said, "I can't imagine anyone better equipped to do a job for Seacraft."

I believe I know new prospects for you from Maine to Florida. And I know your boat from stem to stern.

Later in the week I will telephone you to arrange a personal meeting at your convenience. I would like to discuss further how and why I think I can help boost Seacraft sales this year.

Yours truly,

George Frasier

Box 72
Larchmont, New York 10538
914–113–2626

A RECENTLY WIDOWED MOTHER OF TWO TEEN-AGERS CONVERTS A
PRIVATE-LIFE INTEREST INTO A PAY JOB WITH THIS LETTER

Mr. James W. Forsythe, President
Duro-Style Chinaware, Inc.
Stamford, Conn. 06901

Dear Mr. Forsythe:

I think you design and manufacture the most interesting variety of durable quality china on the national market.

As the wife of a professional city manager who has served in three separate areas of the country, it has been my "business" to entertain men and women from many walks of life.

I have three different settings of Duro-Ware and take a special pride in using it properly.

I have been "talking" Duro-Ware to my guests for twenty years and have helped a number of friends and acquaintances select and buy the right thing for their particular needs.

In the last four years I have lectured on table settings before approximately fifty women's clubs and church and civic groups.

Now I want to convert this experience to demonstrating, individual counseling, and public speaking for your fine product.

I would like to show you some professionally made color slides of table settings using Duro-Ware which have been enthusiastically received by my audiences, and I would like to discuss further how what I know about your products can be put to profitable use for you.

I will be pleased to drive down to Camden to see you. A week from today I will telephone you long distance to learn when an appointment can be arranged at your convenience.

Yours truly,

Mrs. Ella Rogers

Glen Road
Winchester, Mass. 01890

A NEW AMERICAN WITH MODERATE EXPERIENCE IN GERMANY
GETS HIS FIRST JOB HERE WITH THIS LETTER THREE WEEKS
AFTER ARRIVAL IN THIS COUNTRY

Mr. George Menkin
Dock Street
Yonkers, New York 10701

I have learned of your shop operation and I like the sound of the way you people do things. I want to work for you.

I have a good mechanical background with a degree in engineering and experience with problems like yours—the design and modification of hydraulic equipment.

As supervisor of a small design team for a hydraulic press factory in Germany, I directed the detail designing and calculation of all-welded machine frames for presses up to 2000 tons capacity.

I designed a pneumatically-operated ram locking device for a hydraulic die-spotting press which could be installed as a complete unit, thus cutting down installment costs 30%.

My design of a hydraulic circuit to operate a movable working table was adopted by the company as standard design. And I have resolved problems of high pressure seals up to 5,000 pounds per square inch.

I am familiar with American design too, as I have been called upon several times to remodel them to meet the needs and facilities of European manufacturers.

I would like to show you more about how I have handled these assignments and how, as a member of your design team, I can help work out the problems you are facing every day.

Tuesday morning I will telephone you at your shop to find out when it will be most convenient for you to see me.

Yours truly,

Thomas Huldschiner

356 West 34th St.
New York, New York 10001
212–733–4896

In these last three letters, it is important for you to realize what was omitted.

The "boat man" once had a physical handicap which made it impossible for him to work full time in his earlier adult years. Now he is cured. Actually, he had no real employment story to tell. And, to top that, he was known in boating circles as a rich man though he had just suffered a serious financial setback.

The woman with the dishes had been very recently widowed. She had two teen-agers to support and they would limit extensive travel which might be called for in the job she's after.

The young engineer-designer had just arrived in the United

States. He had a thick accent and no employment experience in
this country at all.

Notice that none of these job finders went into a long story
which would make their personal problems the employer's problems and wave a caution flag in front of the man doing the
hiring. Also, none of these applicants puts himself on the defensive by involving the personal matters and trying to "explain
away" anything. Instead, these letters adhere strictly to that
part of the authors' experience, background, and interests which
spell out specific benefits to the prospects.

Be careful that your letters stick to the point this way, especially if you haven't had the practice of working out a résumé.
Now, start writing.

Don't worry if you can't fit every one of the prescribed elements into your circumstances. There is no such thing as a
perfect job-finding letter. If you do the best you can and if you
manage to get most of the foregoing suggested elements into
your letter, it will probably get the results you want. When you
finish, you will find it helpful to refer to the following check list.
Although this list is not designed for your type of letter, it does
include many features which you will want to consider in composing the best possible letter.

Check List for an Introductory Letter to Accompany a Resume

1. Does your letter look brief and is it neat?

2. Is the employer's name spelled correctly?

3. Have you written his title properly?

4. Is your opening remark not more than five lines?

5. Is it a factual matter rather than your opinion?

6. Is it really pertinent to your application?

7. Have you indicated scope in specific numbers?

8. Have you enlarged a little on one but not more than two phases of your experience?

9. Have you indicated that the résumé is enclosed or attached?

10. Have you included one or not more than two abbreviated examples from your résumé?

11. In abbreviating the résumé examples, have you retained the most significant facts in each?

12. Have you asked for the job and told the employer you want to work for him?

13. Have you asked for the appointment?

14. Have you worded the appointment request positively so that the next move is in your control?

15. Have you mentioned one but no more than two of your employers' names?

16. Have you selected the names which have the most meaning for the person you are addressing?

17. Have you limited yourself to just one employer-quote, if any?

18. Have you avoided explaining away your personal circumstances?

19. Have you avoided flattery, oversolicitousness, and exaggerated expressions of gratitude?

CHAPTER XII

How to Use the Telephone to Your Advantage

Should you call or wait for him to call? What you can learn from the secretary. Are you being interviewed without your knowledge?

The first thing to command about telephone calls is, "Make them." We are continually surprised at the number of job campaigners who dive unhesitatingly into their research, résumés, and letters, but won't pick up a telephone. They'll go back to the résumé and reword a little phrase. They'll compose another good letter. They'll rearrange a detail in their portfolios, *anything* to postpone making the call.

Some confess that they're sort of embarrassed or afraid they'll get a "No" answer. It isn't logical to feel a personal embarrassment because your relationship with the employer is not personal. You're not trying to make love. You're proposing to make money for him. You're not attempting to take his time and burden him. You are calling to suggest that your experience can save him time and relieve him of burdens.

He may be deluged with applications. But if your résumé and letter were composed properly, they've probably been received as a welcome relief from the mass of mail that comes over his desk. You'll get some "no" answers, of course. Everyone does. But if you've followed our suggestions, you have a number of prospects so that the success of your campaign doesn't hinge on any single call. In fact, if your job hunt depends on one call, something other than the telephone is the barrier. Check back over your research. Then pick up the phone with renewed vigor. True, it might be like diving into cold water and you may still

150

wish to hesitate. But after that first plunge, it will probably feel good.

When you make your calls, plan what you will say before you dial. Plan it according to what's going to come from the other end of the line. There are four possibilities: He isn't available at the moment. He says, "Yes." He says, "No." He says, "Maybe."

If he isn't available at the moment, you can still make the call count for something in your discussion with the secretary. No matter what her general instructions may be or how skilled she is in saying nothing politely, you can get helpful clues from her with some casually placed direct questions: Does she recall your résumé and letter? Did her boss read them? If he read them, what does he propose to do about them?

1. Throw them away?

2. Hold them for a couple of days or a week?

3. Arrange an interview now?

Will he be especially busy in the next few days? If so, for how many days? When would it be most convenient for him to receive another call from you? Early in the morning at nine o'clock? Just before or after lunch at about noon or two-thirty? Or late in the afternoon after five? "Thank you I'll call again. Good-by."

Don't fire your questions as rapidly as this. But these are the useful specifics you can gain from talking with his secretary, if he hasn't already instructed her to arrange an appointment for you. Keep in mind that it's the employer you're trying to make a date with, not his secretary. Treat her as a friend, for she can indeed be a good one at this time. Remember, she has the key to the sanctum. Don't give her time to jump the gun and put you on an indefinite waiting line with, "Don't call us. We'll call you." If she asks if you wouldn't like *him* to call you back, thank her graciously and explain that you don't mind calling. You're going to be in and out so much that you might miss his message.

If the employer agrees to see you, set a date then and there.

If it's his secretary you are addressing and she doesn't have the power to make the appointment on the spot, tell her you'll call back. And have an understanding about what time you'll call. You control the situation.

If he says, "No," was it a flat "No"? Or was it projected in a way so as to imply "Maybe"? If you're sure it was a final "No," forget it and call the next number. But very possibly he meant "Maybe."

If he says, "Maybe," he means either that your timing isn't just right and he's not quite ready for you, or he's thought about your application and hasn't decided on what to do about it yet. In either instance, it's almost certain that he wants you to give him a little more reason why a meeting with you would be worth his time. This is the situation for which you must be ready, preferably with written notes alongside the phone. You may have to fire a couple of your best leading questions right then and there to get him talking about himself. Think about his problems and what you can produce for him. He may actually cue you into some thoughts about why he has his doubts, just to find out what you'll say. In any event, talk your points in résumé language and hit him hard with those results, facts, and figures.

Perhaps, in this case, you failed to line up your résumé functions in the order of his particular needs, or possibly there's a qualification for this job which you have but neglected to mention in your résumé. Could it be that you de-emphasized something which is important to him? Is there a phase of your background which he needs to know more about?

Ask him some direct questions about this sort of specific detail. If the conversation runs over four minutes, be aware that you're actually having an interview. You're being screened on the telephone without possibly realizing it. Pick up his leads and then follow the same interview procedures prescribed at the end of this book. Keep it going until either you or he can naturally say, "This sounds interesting. Why don't we get together?" And make a date.

CHAPTER XIII

How to Get Ready and Pack for the Interview

Three kinds of useful notes. Some interview traps.
What about references? When to use samples.
That delicate personal situation. For men. For women.

Whether you carry a handbag, an attaché case, or a slightly soiled manila envelope, there are some useful items you'll want to take with you to your interview.

If you've followed this book in working out your research and preparing job-finding tools, you are well aware that each of your interviews will call for a decidedly individual approach. By interview time, your career and job decisions should be sufficiently determined so that you don't swing and sway with the wind from one interviewer and another. *You* remain constant. Your prospective employers, on the other hand, will change from one interview to the next. Each has his own special interests. Each one operates within a different organizational framework.

Review the information which you've gathered on your prospects. In every case, what are the particular circumstances and how does your background apply to them? If you don't have an organized file, compose a few key notes to take along in your interview luggage. Don't count on your memory.

One employer may make a practice of keeping his first interview with every applicant very short. This kind of screening session can end very abruptly. In the rush, you may forget some of your best selling points if you don't have them itemized on paper for quick reference.

Another interviewer may force you unexpectedly down a long

side track and then suddenly begin to look at his watch. You have four minutes to save a lost cause and to get to your points. It will take some carefully prepared cue notes to build a strong, hard-sell finale in a situation like this.

Three Kinds of Useful Interview Notes

There are three separate sets of notes which you'll need for a productive interview. Two of these contain leading questions.

One type of leading question is designed expressly for coaxing your interviewer to talk about himself and his problems, his favorite subjects and, incidentally, his vulnerable spots. Remember, he knows quite a lot about you from your résumé and letters. You can now establish a more equal footing if you find out more about him.

Think of yourself as a reporter preparing for an interview with a celebrity. Your livelihood depends on your ability to make that person talk. What are the subjects close to his heart? Write out three specific questions. Write them because you'll word them more effectively. Make them specific because you won't get anywhere discussing generalities. Compose three questions because the first two might not work.

Use your research to form the questions, that article about him which you found in *Fortune* magazine, his last year's convention speech which you discovered in a trade association office, the recent story about his organization's newest plans which you read in one of the trade publications.

If you asked a young mother how much her baby weighed and, "Is the baby on solids yet?," you wouldn't have much trouble getting an expansive answer. And once she had opened up you could lead casually from your original question into more revealing inquiry. Your prospective employer has his "babies" too, his pet theories, his burdens of the moment. The best way to come out of the interview with the job is to convey the impression that you can make yourself a helpful, profitable part of his nine-to-five life. The right coaxing questions will give you an excellent start.

The second kind of leading question is the type which is used casually to indicate your knowledge of the field and understanding of the employer's problems.

If you were to ask a house painter, "What kind of paint do you use on exterior siding?," you would not in any way suggest that you knew the first thing about paint. But if you asked him, "What is your thinking about the latex breather paints as against the flat alkyd type for exteriors where there's a moisture problem?," he would immediately recognize that you knew something about the subject.

Whatever your field or level may be, you can project the same kind of questions for the same strategic purpose. Again, for practice sake, write three of these questions. Be especially mindful about the specifics here because generalities won't serve the purpose at all. Frame the questions so as to leave the answer open to your interviewer's judgment. And be careful not to express your inquiry in a way that implies you have some unbending, pre-conceived idea of the correct answer which might be contrary to your interviewer's strong feelings in the matter.

After you have planned leading questions centered around your prospective employer's point of view, you will do well to work out a third category of direct questions having to do with your own interests.

These are questions designed to acquire the insight it will take to make your personal decision. Of course, some of the information you need will automatically come from your leading questions. But if this is left to chance, you're likely to find yourself halfway home and suddenly realizing that there's one decisively important detail which never came up at all. You won't be caught this way if you have a check list to summarize the interview.

In composing your direct questions, be sure to word them enthusiastically, positively, and courteously—perhaps even casually—so your interviewer doesn't get the impression that you're more interested in what you can get than what you can give.

We won't attempt to itemize your list of questions because you know what you want better than we do. But here are three basic considerations you should be sure not to overlook.

First, you can probably use some more specific information regarding your prospect's future plans and how they may affect the job at stake. And while you're contemplating the future, you might discern a little more about the past.

If a new job is being created, what are the circumstances which led to this? If you are replacing somebody, how long was your predecessor on the job. If he was there only three months, it could mean that the employer is a poor judge of candidates or perhaps he isn't describing the job as it actually is. If your predecessor worked on that job fifteen years, he may have been a very good man and a hard one to follow. Or there could have been some sudden internal shake-up which might be good or bad for you. Or, for any number of reasons, your predecessor could have found a better job somewhere else. Maybe you can too.

Second, after your prospect discloses he's definitely interested in you, it's important to know whom you'd be working with and for. Be especially mindful of this if your interviewer is someone other than the person you'd be working with. No matter how much confidence you and the interviewer may have in each other, you could be assigned to someone else with whom you do not share the same mutual respect. In some instances, you might not see the interviewer again for months; if it's a large organization, maybe *never*.

Then, there's that vital question about your salary. For the moment, your need is to make ready for attack with specific figures. We're not attempting to tell you how to bargain. But the employer has his figures in mind and if you don't have yours, you won't have any equipment to spar with.

Begin your figuring with an estimate of your own personal

irreducible minimum. Regardless of what the job is or who the employer might be, what is the least income you must have to fill your obligations? Decide this first and stick to your decision if you want any assurance of lasting enjoyment in your new job.

Next, how much money will you ask of each particular prospective employer in each individual situation? This may take a little more research.

You might make another broad check with the Help Wanted and Business Opportunities sections of your most accessible large city newspapers and with the trade publications. But, of course, you can determine only the general pay ranges from these sources. And there can be a considerable difference from one of your prospects to the next.

If you're headed for a job in a non-profit field, the salary scale will depend largely on whether the organization is financed by an endowment or is dependent upon the vagaries of annual memberships and contributions. In commercial fields, there are many more variables which make the difference. The price tag in the same type of a job can differ from one company to the next although they are the same general kind and size of operation, in practically the same market, with a similar volume, and nearly the same Dun & Bradstreet rating.

Some companies are popularly known in their trade as "good pay," others as "fair pay," others as "below average." Where does each of your prospects fit in this scale? You'll have to do still more detective work to find out. Maybe you can feel out the trade and professional organizations and publications on this detail. Go back to your research interview man. Ask him what he knows or can find out for you on the going prices. Then arrive at a figure as reasonably close as possible to what each individual prospect might or will pay.

If there's any question about this, make it a little bit high rather than too low. Employers are known to reject applicants who ask for too little, for if your stated money requirement is below the top level of your résumé, your prospects have good reason to doubt that you're actually as good as you claim. You have set a good pace in your résumé. Don't slow it down by hesitating to ask for reward which is commensurate with that level. If you were to ask for an amount very much less than the employer has objectively estimated for that job, he might get the idea that he should reappraise the whole situation. Perhaps he should look around for other candidates who are really up to the caliber of the predetermined salary level.

Finally, think of the way in which your personal needs appear to your prospects. If your résumé indicates a fairly substantial-sounding address and specifies "Married, four children," the employer will think something's out of order if you don't demand that kind of money. He might reject you on the grounds that you'd be discontented with less income than it obviously takes to maintain your present standard of living. Or he might guess you have an independent income and don't need to work very badly. In either case, you wouldn't be a safe bet for a long-run job.

No matter what your field, your level, or personal circumstances may be, and regardless of how anxious you are to get that job, never try to make a selling point of asking for a relatively small amount of money. This procedure doesn't work because it gives rise to all sorts of suspicions as to what goes on behind your curtain. Maybe you can and will settle for less to get the job. Just don't plan this as any kind of an initial sales tool.

Contrary to popular complaints, employees are usually paid approximately what they are worth according to the particular needs of a particular organization. If you have followed the suggestions in this book, you have concentrated your principal efforts on research to discover that particular situation for you. If you've found the prospects who need you, you undoubtedly are worth more money to them than you have been to your previous employers. Prepare to ask for it before you go to each interview.

References

We have suggested that you do not include a list of references with your initial mailing of résumés or letters. Such a list, particularly a long one, introduced at this early stage might appear as if you were on the defensive. What is more, you may have good reason to select different references for different prospects.

Some small or medium-sized employers may never ask you for any references at all. They prefer to find out what they can directly from you. Other organizations of the same size will ask you for references just to see if you are hesitant to produce them. Some of these employers will insist upon references and then never use them. Even if you give a certain prospective employer the phone number of a mutual acquaintance, he might not use it because he doesn't want his friend to know he's looking for an employee. And if that friend is a competitor, maybe your prospect doesn't want him to know that you are available.

But practically all large employers and some smaller ones will ask for references as a routine procedure. In your interview you may be called upon to furnish three names. Have them ready.

Make your references count for more than simply verifying your admirable character. Select people who can substantiate the claims in your résumé and add a little more impact to your application. If the most important function in your résumé is "Supervising Personnel", use a reference who knows about your ability at this function.

Before you use any name, contact that person for permission to do so. This is not only a courtesy, but also gives you a chance to brief your reference so he'll understand how to help you. If it's a good friend, you can suggest specifics for him to mention when he is called to speak in your behalf. Just be sure he's not too obvious about them.

Every employer knows perfectly well that you aren't intentionally going to volunteer references who will not speak well for you. There is a certain kind of snooping employer who might contact your good references to see if, through them, he can find others who might not be so sympathetic to your cause. Then, of course, every name mentioned in your résumé is a potential reference. Even if your résumé refers only to an organization, your prospective employers can call that organization to find out who knows you.

No matter how devious your prospects may be in this detail, they are unlikely to make any third-party inquiry until they've seen you in person. You can straighten out any serious concern you have about the matter in the interview.

If you don't want your present employer to know you're looking for another job, it's perfectly legitimate to advise your prospects of this without elaborating. If you're pretty sure that one of your past employers will not speak well for you, be prepared to tell your prospect what he's going to hear before he hears it from somebody else. Explain the circumstances briefly. Don't however, introduce the matter and give rise to suspicion unless it's really necessary.

For practice sake, try writing your explanation so you can edit it to eliminate defensiveness and criticism of the other fellow. A good way to phrase it is simply "We (you and your employer) were unable to work together productively because I felt . . . etc." Then continue to cite positively what it was you "felt." If you're careful how you word this, you can illustrate something about the way you do things which will represent a favorable point to your prospect.

We do not want to suggest that your prospective employers are a group of supersleuths who will use all sorts of cunning tricks to dig up dirt about you. The vast majority will do no such thing. In fact, there is usually a gentlemen's understanding that any job application is a confidential matter, especially if you are employed at the time. Most employers will respect your privacy. Our principal reason for calling attention to the possible hazards is that sometimes an employer will mention your availability unintentionally. If you're prepared for it, you won't get in trouble.

Most applicants are needlessly apprehensive about word of

their job hunt leaking to the wrong person. It's true that if you get "caught" by your current employer, it may cause a little unpleasantness. But that's all. Even in the rare instance when an employee is supposedly fired just because he's discovered looking for another job, the incident is usually only a last straw on a pile of undesirable conditions which the applicant is better off without.

Don't worry too much about that reference who's not going to speak favorably of you. The criticism of one man from all your former associates isn't likely to do harm if other people speak highly of you.

In any event, if you want a better job you have to attack full force without hesitating just because you're afraid somebody is going to find out what you're up to. You have to expose your wares if you want to sell them. You must name organizations and individuals which represent the best names for yours to be associated with.

Illustrative Materials

Whether you pack an over-sized art case, a portable file of writings, a pocket folder of business papers, or possibly a kit full of inventions to illustrate your capabilities, follow these three rules: stick to the point; make it look like you; and cut it in half.

Stick to the point by following the continuity of your résumé exactly. Compile your illustrations according to each functional heading. Start with the first and most important function and continue with each one you want to illustrate in order of its consequence to the individual prospect. This is the easiest way to make law and order of your portfolio because you already have the outline to follow. Also, it is the simplest way to talk about your samples in the interview because you have practiced your talk in writing the résumé.

Most importantly, your samples must count for something more than decoration. When you line them up with your résumé, they become the positive proof of your claims rather than a hodge-podge collection of pictures, reprints, or tear sheets. Think of your sample kit or presentation as a visual sales aid. One good way to make it sell you is to begin each section with printed or free-hand headlines quoting your résumé functions verbatim. You can take an effective step farther by adding smaller type sub-headings of excerpts from your résumé quoting several of your "results" as they apply to each visual illustration.

Make it look like you by constructing the whole presentation as you would ordinarily do things in your regular work routine.

If you are in an art field, your visual presentation should represent the character of your day-to-day work at its best. The binder, the paper, the color, the copy, the materials, the whole thing should be your style as you usually produce it. If you are in a technical field, your sample kit, the objects, photos, and descriptions should be as precise as the nature of your occupation. If you are a business man, your illustrative materials should be businesslike, neat, and clear.

But whether your work is most appropriately illustrated within an originally designed, colored cloth binder or a stationery-store folder of acetate sleeves, don't make it too fancy. Like those gimmicked-up résumés, the over-done sample kit can look artificial or give the impression that you must be hard up to go to all that extra trouble. And ironically, if you do an especially beautiful job of putting together and labeling your illustrative materials, you can create a production which distracts from the subject. Remember you are concerned with only one subject; that job. Don't make your presentation an eye-catcher. Make it a job-getter.

One of our Forum men in a field of artistic design devoted weeks to preparing as elaborate a presentation as we've ever seen. It was a thing of beauty and perfection. In fact, every time he was interviewed, his presentation created such a favorable impression that the interviewer rang interoffice phones to invite company officials to see the magnificent display. Congratulations and compliments ran rampant. But the closing remarks of the interviewer were always, "You certainly have a lot of ability of some sort. I wish we could find a place to use it in our organization." One interviewer actually said, "This is a beautiful and forceful piece of work. You should get a job some place making presentations." Our designer friend's masterpiece was illustrating his qualifications for "Creating and Producing Visual Presentations." Unfortunately, however, this was not one of the functions of the job he was applying for.

Don't distract your prospects with an overdone visual demonstration which stands alone by itself rather than complementing your other job-finding tools.

Cut it in half by following the same method you employed to select your résumé examples. If you have a sample that proves you're qualified to lift a hundred pounds, do not include another sample of the same kind which suggests that you can also lift fifty pounds.

And, as always, keep that employer and his problems in mind. If you invented a new kind of mousetrap, you may be justifiably proud of it. Show it to your friends. But don't take it along to your job interviews unless your prospect is in the exterminating business and needs an employee who specializes in mice.

There's nothing that scares interviewers more than a job applicant who walks in with a trunk full of scrap book scraps. If you enter the office burdened with a fat case of samples, your interviewer may think, "I don't want any," before you start to sell. He may suspect that you're all over the lot if it takes that much stuff to make your point. He doesn't need a trunk full of ideas to clutter his office. He only needs one thing that works and will solve his problem.

If you have a specific reason to carry along extras in case your prospect should ask for them, place them in a pocket in back of your presentation or in a separate thin envelope. Don't water down the impact of your visual story by inserting these "doubtfuls" in the middle of your direct message. Pack light for your interview if you want to shed light on your qualifications.

That Delicate Personal Situation

You think you're too old or too young?

You've been unemployed for a long while?

You were fired from your last job?

You walked out on an employer?

You've been a free-lancer all your working life?

You've been in the family business, never really on your own?

You've had your own business which failed?

You're a woman applying for a man's work?

You're a man without wife or family?

You have a physical or emotional handicap?

You have some other skeleton in your closet?

If you are suffering from one of the above common afflictions, unless it is a very serious physical handicap, you have probably magnified it out of all realistic proportion. Now, before you go to your next interview, is the time to resolve it.

"But," you insist, "employers have already told me my 'affliction' was against me. So, of course, it's very real."

That may be what you were told. But that is probably not the reason you didn't get the job. To begin with, employers don't often reject an applicant because of one single feature in the job-hunter's background. The rejection is made for multiple and subtle reasons, often involving inside matters which you either haven't taken the trouble to find or couldn't have learned in advance. As employers don't choose to go into a long explanation, they reach for the most convenient answer. That answer is the easiest way out for them. But, for you, it can be like scratching an old sore. Just consider the source.

Even if one employer does really mean that your affliction is the reason you've been turned down, it probably isn't so much the affliction itself as it is what you have made of it in the interview. It isn't because you're too old; it's because you're old-thinking. It isn't because you've been out of work for a while; it's because you think unemployed. It isn't because you failed in your own business; it's because you talk failure. And it isn't because you have some other skeleton in the closet. It's because you insist on reminding yourself and your prospects that the skeleton is there.

Forget yourself and think of it from the employer's point of view. He needs your assets. He can't use your liabilities. He's concerned about his problems, not yours. His primary purpose in the interview is to find out what you can do for him with your good qualifications, not what you can't do for him because of some liability. If you center the discussion around how your valuable experience can serve him profitably, he's not going to spend interview time searching for a fly in the ointment.

But a lot of us are not experts in controlling conversation. That "delicate matter" could possibly slip into the discussion. It's advisable to have your answer ready so you can go to the interview more confident and relaxed.

The best answer you can give is the truth. We remind you that no matter how clever a fable you may have, the records show you're almost certain to be caught. Even if your story does get you the job, you're probably on borrowed time. You'll most likely be looking for another job when the truth becomes known, whether or not you have built a good performance record in the interim.

We've seen employers and employees try to patch things up after the lie is detected. They string along together for a while. But an exposed interview lie hangs around the office like an old clock that can't be depended on because it stopped once. Finally, somebody says, "Let's get rid of this thing and find a new one."

In common sense language, employers don't like to assign responsibilities to people they can't trust. So, if you insist that you have some realistic job affliction like those we've mentioned, work out a clear, honest answer. Employers do like to assign responsibility to people they trust. Your forthright honesty about a delicate issue is a pretty sure sign that your word is good. The matter which you're worrying about could just as well become a credit as a disqualification.

Plan what you will say. Word it in the most positive way possible. Then forget it! Take it along "for emergency only."

At Least Two Copies of Your Résumé

Some interviewers won't refer to your résumé in conversation at all. But others will follow it point by point. And it may have been mislaid.

When you arrive you may discover more than one interviewer, and you'll want to have enough résumés to go around. The additional interviewers may be last-minute guests who don't know the first thing about you. It will be easier if they have your résumé in front of them. So before you close your interview luggage, carefully place at least two copies in a spot where you can reach them fast. Make certain it is the same résumé which you sent to the employer who's about to interview you. Read it over once more to refresh your memory on the points most applicable to his needs.

Just as your résumés, letters, and phone calls should sound like you at your best, you should look your best at the interview. This is the first thing your prospect sizes up when you walk in and the last thing he notices as you leave.

You've put a lot of thought and effort into arriving at this interview. Don't throw it away by carelessly overlooking something as simple as your appearance. Take two minutes to read these next few paragraphs even if you think you have this matter well in hand.

If you are in a field having anything to do with dress or grooming, you are the expert and you know what's best. Realize that details of your appearance are a sample of your work just as the writing in a copy writer's résumés and letters are samples of his skill. And if you work in technical research or in one of the creative fields, you should, though it may be contrary to your feelings, curb individuality in dress so as not to suggest that you are too far "out" to fit into a routine work-a-day world with the rest of the employees, not to mention the customers and clients.

But, for most of us, appearance is a matter of applying a little soap and water, taking care to look neat, and remembering to dress for a business meeting, not for a ball or a beach party.

In the following paragraphs we are not attempting to advise you as to what is good taste. That is a matter for your individual opinion. If the prescribed apparel and grooming is so far removed from your regular getup that it would make you uneasy, forget it and wear what makes you feel relaxed and confident.

For men. Some menswear fashions go to extremes which may possibly be appropriate for people in your line of work. You are the best judge of that. But usually you can't go far wrong by leaning at least moderately toward the conservative side. Most importantly, make sure your apparel is clean and pressed. Think twice about five–o'clock shadow and a mussy necktie. Realize that if you have occasion to move alongside your interviewers and thumb through some papers with them, your hands and fingernails will be very conspicuous. Give yourself an inspection from neat hair to shoeshine before each interview. You can be sure your interviewers will do so.

For Women. You may want to vary your appearance somewhat depending on the type of job for which you are applying. A flamboyant, high-fashion look may impress an interviewer at an advertising agency or a designer clothing salon but would be inappropriate for an accounting firm or bank. However you choose to dress, it is important that you feel comfortable and look neat. If you walk clumsily in your high-styled shoes or feel awkward in your fashionable new hat that you're unaccustomed to wearing, you will present a clumsy, awkward appearance. Remember, too, that if you're hired while wearing a simple silk shirtwaist dress and show up for your first day of work in jeans and a T-shirt, your employer has every right to think that you were being deceptive.

As for accessories and makeup, avoid the vulgar and ostentatious. Don't wear jewelry if you're not used to it. If you unconsciously start fiddling with an earring or bangle bracelets, you'll appear nervous and apprehensive. Wearing more makeup than you usually do or a radically different hairstyle might also make you feel uneasy. In general, try to avoid wearing anything that's a substantial departure from your own personal style. The more comfortable you feel, the more confident you'll be. Knowing that you look well will help you put yourself across in the best possible way.

Get everything ready the night before so you won't have to rush in the morning when you have other important business details to concentrate on. Check again quickly just before you enter the building where you're having the interview. Do not count on making last-minute personal repairs in the elevator. The person standing next to you may be the one who's going to interview you.

Incidentally, some of our Forum women have found it convenient to make a note of their appearance at each interview so that they avoid looking the same in another follow-up interview with the same man. And, if you're unwed but still working on it, more power to you. But don't exercise it in the way you appear for your interviews if you want a job which represents any kind of temporary security. In this particular instance, you're looking for a job, not a man. And it is important to convey the impression that you're from the working world, not from finishing school or from the kitchen. Dress and groom accordingly.

Now you are equipped with interview notes on the three types of questions you're going to use, a list of references, illustrative materials (if any), the answer to that delicate situation, and extra copies of your résumé. Your clothes are mended and clean. You're ready to go.

CHAPTER XIV

The Lively Art of Interviewing

What to listen for and what to talk about.
Opening the conversation.
Difficult questions.
Interruptions.
Those silent humps.
Unexpected guests.
Sample work on speculation.

Every suggestion in this book is planned with one primary goal in mind, your success in the interview. If you have carefully followed each step, you're better prepared to sell yourself than the vast majority of your competitors.

Remember that employers need good employees just as urgently as you need a good job. They want to see you. Most of them feel it will be to their advantage to extend a courteous reception and a fair hearing. But some will play a little rough. If you're prepared for the worst, you'll do your best in any circumstances.

You could be challenged with a situation like this:

The employer lounges in a luxurious swivel chair behind a big solid desk. There are some little seats strategically placed out in front of the desk.

The job applicant, neatly dressed and carrying light luggage, walks in briskly despite a thirty-minute wait outside in the reception room. The employer is busy on a long-distance telephone. As he barks into the phone, he waves applicant to one particular little seat.

The phone conversation continues five more minutes. The

employer hangs up and fires consecutively, "How do you do?" "What do we have to discuss?" "What can I do for you?"

The applicant replies, "Well . . . er . . . ah . . . you have my résumé. Perhaps you'd like to . . .."

The employer interrupts. He buzzes for his secretary and orders her to bring in a jury.

The applicant continues, "I was saying that perhaps you'd like to read my résumé and then I can answer any questions you might have."

The employer explains that he's looked at so many résumés lately he doesn't remember which is which, and he doesn't have a copy of the particular résumé in front of him anyway.

The applicant dives into luggage for résumé as jury enters and is introduced one by one. Extra résumé copies are distributed, but the employer rules, "Let's not bother with them. You just tell us all about yourself."

The applicant wrings his résumé copy into a stick and begins, "Well . . . er . . . mmmm . . .."

Situations like this do happen to the best of job applicants—not infrequently. And you may find yourself suddenly in the middle of just such a scene. But you can steal the show if you know your lines and are ready for any kind of audience.

To begin with, if you have any personal feeling of apprehension or uneasiness before the curtain goes up, take solace in the fact that your interview is not a social get-together. It's a business conference. And there's a lot of difference.

The interviewer isn't concerned only with your personality. He's a buyer or purchasing agent searching out the best material he can find for a certain price. He wants to find out what you can do for him and his organization from nine to five. His mind is on his bank book, not on the color of your eyes.

Next, consider the interviewer. There are roughly three categories of interviewers—the self-made old hand at sizing up job applicants, the inexperienced recruiter, and the professional personnel expert.

If your interviewer is a self-made old hand, he may be a little impatient, discourteous, and short with you like the employer in the previous scene. But remember that no matter how aloof or disgruntled he may act, he found something he liked in your résumé. Dig for that something and pound the table just as hard as he does if you wish. Overlook his act. You may find that he is actually the easiest to deal with because he'll come to the point quickly and let you know just where you stand with him.

If the person behind the desk is inexperienced in the art of interviewing, he may be quite vague and perhaps lingering in his approach. But he too has looked over your résumé and found something he liked although he may not have made up his mind about what he wants. Or perhaps he doesn't know how to describe what he wants. It's up to you to help this man make conversation. Find out that "something" he liked. Help him make up his mind in your favor.

If your interviewer is a professional personnel expert, recognize that his position is to hire people, not reject them. His annual report must show a good ratio between the number of people he spends company time interviewing and the number of productive employees he hires. He has scrutinized your résumé carefully. Unlike the inexperienced recruiter, the trained personnel man knows exactly what to look for and he's found some particulars of special interest in your background. Feel him out and listen for the specifics he has in mind. Then you can enlighten him further with regard to the things he's interested in.

Whatever kind of interviewer you face from one prospect to the next, keep in mind that he has definite reasons to suspect you have something to offer him or he wouldn't have made the appointment.

The first thing to watch might be the length of time he keeps you waiting in the reception room. Five to not more than fifteen minutes is average. If he holds you out for a half hour or more, don't let your aggravation cloud the issue. An extra long wait may indicate something you'll want to consider calmly in making your choice of jobs.

What caused the wait? Was it because the employer was short of help and urgently needs the kind of relief you can offer him? If so, capitalize on it. Show him you can fill his needs and you're ready to produce for him. Was it because the employer is inefficient, unorganized, or just plain inconsiderate? If so, you're probably not going to change him. Perhaps you'd better follow up your next prospect, the one who won't keep you waiting either now or later when you're on the job.

Once you get inside, no matter how gracious or how curt the reception may be, you come to the point first—if this can be managed. Try not to force him or even allow him to be the one who introduces the business of the meeting. If you can beat him to the punch, you've won the first point.

Have your lead line ready. All you need is a pleasant, genuine expression of your interest and enthusiasm for his organization and the job at stake. Keep your opening remarks general until you've had time to feel him out. You might hit a wrong note by jumping to a specific item at the outset.

One of our Forumites found newspaper mention of a prospective employer's plans for moving to offices in a new and beautiful building. The applicant thought this a natural conversation item and opened the interview by offering his congratulations. But the new offices turned out to be a very sore subject with his particular interviewer and started him off in the wrong frame of mind. He used nearly five minutes of the limited interview time expressing his profound disapproval of the location, the rent, the interior decoration, and the elevator system. Then he said indignantly, "This has nothing to do with our meeting. Get to the subject."

Don't lose five important selling minutes this way. Your opening remark need only be a casual "I'm interested" sort of thing, just some little introduction to show that you want to get down to business. But, of course, you can't always win this round.

There's an interviewer who'll start right off in his own defense. As you walk in the door, he'll hold up his hand and warn you that he has no job opening. Ignore this completely, no matter how he explains it. If he didn't need help or anticipate a need in the very near future, he probably wouldn't have any reason to be talking with you. He couldn't afford the time. Just proceed as scheduled. He probably wants you to sell him on the idea that he could use an extra hand, perhaps your hand.

Then there's an interviewer who'll start throwing the book at you the minute you're seated. He'll challenge you abruptly with, "What do we have to discuss? What can I do for you?" or "Tell me all about yourself."

To frame a good answer, consider the source of the question. Of course, he knows what you have to discuss. He's perfectly well aware of what he can do for you. And he really doesn't want to know "all about yourself" at all. He's seen your résumé and letters and been sufficiently impressed with them to want to see you. That's his point in firing the questions. He wants to find out if you can speak for yourself as well as your résumé did. He wants you to substantiate your résumé claims and expand. And you are the applicant who can do just that because you wrote the résumé and you wrote it in your language.

Play his own game. Turn the tables on him when he challenges you. Tell him with pleasant tongue in cheek, "I'd like to talk about what I can do for *you*, Mr. Employer," or, "What we have to discuss is how my background and experience can serve you profitably," or, "To save you time, rather than tell you all about myself, why don't I confine the story to that part which represents something I believe you can use."

Then, immediately after you've reversed the perspective, summarize your experience in a scope statement or recite the functional headings of your résumé. But make it brief. You've still got to turn the conversation around to your leading questions and get him to talk. Maybe one of your résumé functional headings will provide a natural lead to your first question. If it does, stop right there and project the question.

He may get around to your résumé eventually and ask you specific questions about a few of your claims. But never assume that because you sent him a good résumé you can sit back and let your written advertisement do the selling for you. It won't. It was designed only as an attention getter and a foot in the door. Regardless of how effective your advance notice may have been, the interview is the point of sale. And, for the time being, you are the salesman.

Get to those leading questions. Make him talk. Don't worry if the first question doesn't do the trick. You have more. Plan the early part of your interview as listening time. Make him talk about his organization, his problems. Don't interrupt him until he's completely finished. Remember, you can talk better after you've heard more.

The first five minutes may set the pace for the whole interview. You set it if you can. We don't mean.you to be offensive about this. And we're not suggesting that you can outsmart a veteran interviewer. But you must have the upper hand some of the time if you're going to come out with the job. And, in most instances, a competent interviewer is glad to have you take the lead and will let you keep it if you make the sense he wants to hear.

As the interview progresses, introduce your second category of leading questions, the ones designed to indicate you know something about the field and to get his opinion. Feed this type of question slowly, one question at a time so he can evaluate each one.

Listen some more. If you set the original pace, let him lead for a few laps while you're saving energy to sprint ahead in the end when it counts most. Think of it a little like a debate where you restrain yourself to accrue notes for the rebuttal when it's your turn to make the last winning points.

Realize that while he's leading, he might toss in some nuisance questions such as: "Why are you leaving your present employer?"

"Why did you leave your last job?" "Did you resign or were you fired?" "Why do you want to make a change now?"

You have no need to fret over this kind of question. When you attack the interview with a forward look centered around your prospect's problems, your interviewer isn't inclined to search backward into your past and hover over incidental items. Beyond that, questions like the above never seem to play a significant part in the final outcome unless your reply indicates something out of the ordinary.

But one interviewer or another is almost certain to introduce this sort of detail if for no other reason than to see how straightforwardly you handle it. Have a logical answer ready so you can dispense it promptly and get back to the real issues. Leave money out of it, even if that is a big part of your reason. Leave it out because that's your problem, and the last thing you want to do at this moment is to make this your prospect's problem.

Don't be overly critical of your past or present employer. If you paint an unfavorable picture of them, you'll only lower your own stature. And your prospect will wonder how you came to be mixed up with them in the first place. Don't go into any critical detail about your fellow workers or your disagreements with them. This will only give rise to suspicion that you don't get along with people.

Simply answer in positive, common-sense logic which suggests some favorable promise to your prospect. You're ready for a bigger challenge. There's a lot which you are equipped to do and want to do now for your prospect. Elaborate if you wish. But make it short. Get the conversation back to his problem before it gets lost in the story of your life.

The first step in coping with interruptions is to be fully aware that they probably will take place. In almost every interview your meeting is very likely to be interrupted once, twice, or maybe several times. And as fate would have it, the worst and most unexpected interference seems to come at exactly the wrong moment.

One of our well-prepared Forumites arranged an interview with the executive vice president of a large corporation with impressive offices high atop a metropolitan skyscraper. The applicant was received with red-carpet attention. The meeting progressed beautifully all the way to the critical point of figuring the detailed budget and salary arrangements. Then the interviewer reached for his favorite pencil and found it missing. Immediately the discussion switched to the lost pencil as the employer searched through his clothing. Finally, he rang for his secretary, whom he knew would fully appreciate that the loss of this particular pencil was an emergency situation. Blotters, papers, telephones, lamps, and chair cushions were turned upside down.

As our friend later reported, "The interviewer apologized and kept insisting that I go on with my story. But his head was half buried in the waste basket and I was addressing dollar signs to his protruded rear. The only way I could save the day was to excuse myself and arrange to come back for another meeting."

Interviewers are known to have their idiosyncrasies and to express them in strange ways which can throw you only if they come as a surprise. Don't be caught unaware. Anything can and does happen in the best of companies. Of course, the usual interruption is far more down to earth than that caused by a missing pencil. But sometimes the ordinary can seem more devastating than the unusual. Maybe the employer is just beginning to open up or you are making your strongest point. There is a peak of enthusiasm. Then his phone rings. Or his secretary or first lieutenant enters with an urgent message. Or perhaps no less than his boss walks into the room unannounced.

You feel like you've fallen off the horse, and maybe you have, especially if it's a long and distracting interruption. But the longer it is, up to a point, the more time you have to prepare your recovery.

If the interviewer was talking at the time of the interruption, work out a summary of the point or points he was making. When he's ready to talk again, don't jump on him immediately. Give him a moment of silence to reorient himself and focus back on you. Then recap what he said to suggest what he had in mind. Be careful not to put words in his mouth or color what he actually said to your own liking.

If you were talking at the time of the interruption, summarize your own thoughts and bring him back to you in the same manner. Think it over carefully. You may be able to say it better the second time. No matter which of you was talking at the moment, the longer the interruption, the further back you'll have to go in your recap. Keep this in mind and keep returning further as the interruption continues.

If it seems an extremely long or distracting interruption, you may have to excuse yourself and offer to return later, like the applicant in the missing-pencil interview. But use this technique only as a last resort. Don't quit too easily. Your offer to leave is an acknowledgement that you are not as important as the person who interrupted. Maybe you're not, but don't give your interviewer the idea that he can juggle you around easily. Don't leave just to suit his convenience. Excuse yourself only in the event that the distraction is so intense that it would probably kill your sale that day. Before you depart, make a definite date to see him again.

If you find you are repeatedly faced with rather long and embarrassing periods of silence from one interview to the next, there's probably something more subtle than your interview technique at fault. You may be talking to the wrong prospects about the wrong things. Look back over your résumé and check your research again.

There are occasions when a good interview can seemingly reach a silent standstill. In some instances, the interviewer might stop talking rather abruptly just to hear you speak for yourself without any conversational coaching from him. Maybe you've allowed him to do all the leading thus far. He's made the first three points. Perhaps he wants to see if you're sufficiently in tune with him to make the next logical point four. If you're not ready to follow his sequence exactly and find yourself at a loss for words, reach back to something he's already said and ask him to expand. Use one of your leading questions. Or, refer to one of your not-yet-discussed résumé functions.

Don't just sit there. Say something, preferably something which proves that you've listened and can chime in the same key. You must take the lead now even if the art of making conversation is not expected from a person who does the kind of work you do. Remember, no matter what your field or line of work may be, for the moment you are a salesman.

Sometimes, rather than stopping abruptly, the interviewer will toss a hint and then pause. He's fishing for something, almost like a child who wants an item he's not supposed to have but hopes it will be offered without his having to ask for it.

The little boy knows you have some chocolate candy in your pocket and hints, "I like candy." You wait a silent moment and he clues you further, "I like *chocolate* candy." You still don't respond; so he tries a more direct approach and needles you with, "What's that you've got in your pocket?" If you continue to remain silent, he moves in still closer and demands, "What's that you've got in your pocket, chocolate candy?"

Many interviewers play just such a cat and mouse game with job applicants. Sometimes they use this technique simply to help you talk. If that's the case, listen carefully and jump on to the first clue you recognize.

Sometimes an interviewer will employ this means to force your hand and make you start something which will serve him advantageously simply because you started it. For example, he may attempt to introduce the subject of salary using the hint method. This can be pretty tricky business.

To begin with, even though his first clues may be quite obvious, wait him out a little bit, silence or no silence. Maybe if the trick doesn't work he'll make the first move. But don't wait too long. He may get tired and quit the game. Realize that he's probably had a lot more practice at this than you have.

Whether the subject is salary or some other delicate matter, you may have to lead. Make your lead direct and as brief as possible. Then the next move must be his and maybe you will have the advantage.

If you are applying for an executive position or any job which requires working with and supervising people under pressure, it's natural for your interviewer to test you by applying a little pressure. At some point or several points in the interview he may deliberately attempt to annoy you just to see how you respond.

He may try your patience in the initial wait outside. He may pick up his phone to call a personal friend about a social matter just at the time you're discussing important business. But, he's more likely to interject a thought or question designed to raise your fur. He can search for an inconsequential sensitive spot in your background and try to irritate it. He may explore to find some subject, any subject, concerning which you have a profound opinion and try to rub you the wrong way about it. Some interviewers will even go so far as to sound out your strong political beliefs and coax you along just to see if you'll brew up a storm.

These are common procedures, perfectly fair and logical under the circumstances. Don't fall for them. Just watch them coming and duck. The expert interviewer can slip in this sort of test without your realizing what's going on.

Like most of the interview tricks, the best way to handle this one is to anticipate it. Consider the purpose. Calm down and smile if you find yourself being carried away. If you give the teaser subject a second thought, you'll realize it is probably some issue which has very little if anything to do with the business in point. Come back off the side track and proceed with the interview.

Without any warning, you may be faced with not just one interviewer, but two, three, or even more. They may be there when you walk in. They may be invited in the middle of the session and enter in company formation, or they may drift in and out, one at a time.

Don't be alarmed. This is probably a good sign. If the interviewer is the head man, he's certainly impressed with you if he's willing to command the time of his lieutenants to have them meet you. If your interviewer is a lower echelon screener and calls for the boss, it's a sure sign you're a top candidate. Your only concern is to find out who those other people are. What is their capacity? Have they been previously advised of your application and the purpose of this meeting? And, perhaps most importantly, do they represent potential friends or enemies?

If the master of ceremonies introduces the extra guests and describes their individual positions, see that he does it slowly enough for you to absorb the detail. If you don't quite understand the official status of one guest, interrupt courteously and ask for a repeat definition. If the principal interviewer introduces the others only by name, you have every right to ask what their capacity is. Be tactful and polite in making your inquiry. If it's the lord high executioner, he may be the type who is easily annoyed when people don't recognize his authority and snap to attention. If it's a lieutenant, he's even more likely to be that type. What's more, the lieutenant might be embarrassed to explain who he is in the presence of the boss.

Have the extra guests been familiarized with your application, advised of this meeting and perhaps even instructed as to what their role in it should be? Or have they been nabbed on the spot without having any idea what's going on? In the latter case they'll be very reserved until they discover what it's about and who you are. And the principal interviewer may ask you to orient them just to see how you handle the command.

Are these people potential friends or enemies? Do you represent a gift from heaven in the form of the extra help they've been asking for? Or do you represent a challenge which could threaten one of their jobs? If so, watch out for the daggers and don't talk very much until you know to whom you're talking.

Find out as best you can what their particular interests and problems are and address each person accordingly. Your leading questions may provide an excellent starter. You might have to repeat them and some of the other points you made when the extras weren't present. Don't hesitate simply because it means repetition. You want to cover everybody. And the original interviewer probably liked what you said so it bears repeating.

Finally, realize that the initial interviewer may depart unexpectedly and leave you alone to face the rest of the firing squad. You may find yourself in the middle of a little family group without having the inside advantage of knowing how they feel toward each other. Be careful not to get mixed up in a family argument. If they do get into disagreement among themselves, listen very carefully. This matter may be the best ammunition you can take back to your second interview.

Whatever the circumstances are, and whoever the extra guests may be, their presence on the scene usually means there's something favorable cooking for you. It's up to you to keep the fires burning.

As you approach the end, it is possible that you are fighting the clock without realizing it. You're ready to deliver the *pièce de résistance* which you've saved for the last. You take a deep breath to start; while you're inhaling, the interviewer jumps up and says, "Sorry, I've got to run. We'll let you know. Don't call us, we'll call you. Good-bye."

Obviously you've got to time it better than that. Keep your eye on the clock no matter how well the conversation seems to be going.

You won your first point by beating him to the punch. Win the last one the same way. Before you come too close to the end, watch the interviewer for any little displays of restlessness, like his gathering of papers, glancing at the clock, or sliding toward the front of his chair. If he hasn't indicated the end is in sight, you anticipate it and see how he reacts. Start packing. Sit up straighter. Or stand up if it's that late. Do anything short of blocking the doorway. You mean business. And this is the time to leave no doubt in his mind.

You have listened and made notes for your final points. Come to them before the clock turns your interviewer's mind to his next business of the day.

Maybe your work is of such a nature that your ability and qualifications are best demonstrated by samples. You may question whether or not it's advisable to leave your packet in the hands of a prospect.

The answer is yes providing you leave it for not more than one or two days and have a definite understanding about the time you must retrieve it. If the employer is ready to get down to business, you can force him to review your material in that amount of time. If he, and maybe some other staff member who should see your material, are going to be especially busy for a week or so, this is an excellent cue for you to arrange a follow-up visit.

Simply explain that you'll be pleased to return with your portfolio at a specified time. Make the date on the spot if possible. Or fix it so that you phone him a week from Tuesday.

If the second man will be available in the interim, you might offer to save everybody a little time and trouble by arranging to see him on your own, if that's acceptable.

Your portfolio can be a good tool to pry open doors. Use it. But be careful not to push. Persuade gently. If you have any apprehension about leaving your samples for fear somebody might steal them, forget it. They're not likely to. But even if they were, you'd have to take that chance. As we've warned before, you have to display your wares if you want to sell them.

Should you volunteer to make up a special free sample or write a proposal? The skeptics in this business of job finding will advise you, "Don't do anything for nothing." We disagree not only because our whole premise is based upon "give to receive" but because of the logic that a potential buyer wants to be sure of what he's getting.

In many instances the ability to do a job is best proved by

doing it rather than talking about it. In a situation where there's a new project and a newly created high-level position at stake, the employer may want a written proposal of how you would do it. "What do you promise in writing if elected?" When you volunteer that little extra effort, you have a decisive edge over your competitor for the same job.

By all means, work up that informal proposal, that rough art, the mock-up, the copy, or the design which will effectively demonstrate how you can help your prospect with exactly what he needs. And be wisely aware that such a sample must be based upon specifications of his problem which he will have to spell out for you in *detail* if you're going to make a realistic trial run for him. And these details are more ammunition for you. You will also have the advantage of a follow-up meeting to show your prospect what you've done for him.

Your only reservation in working out special materials for one particular prospect should be the amount of time it will take. If it's a medium-level job, a week or so of your spare time should perhaps be the limit. If it's a top-level job with a long-range possibility, maybe more weeks of your spare time are justifiable.

Just don't get carried away with that one project and that one employer to the neglect of others, especially if it's a long shot. Realize that you can't afford much time on one of these work samples unless you have a specific indication from the employer that you are one of the most likely candidates.

CHAPTER XV

How to Write a Follow-up Letter

Capitalizing on a favorable interview.
Recovering ground after a bad interview.

After the interview, you have a very natural reason to write a follow-up letter of acknowledgment. Don't be oversolicitous in this one. Do not write him, "Thank you for giving me some of your very valuable time last Wednesday. I greatly appreciated the opportunity to talk to you."

Remember again: It's his opportunity you're talking about. It's the value of your time which you're selling. He didn't see you as a big favor. He arranged the interview to find out what you could do for him. And this is what you want to emphasize again in your follow-up letter. Simply lead off, "I was pleased to meet you," or "I enjoyed our visit," or "Thank you for the pleasant lunch." That's enough for social etiquette. Get down to business.

This one letter can be the turn of events. That's just the way it is very often. So before you write, take your time; think it out; plan it carefully. Review the interview completely. Ask yourself the following questions:

Which were the most telltale things he said?

Why do you suppose he said them?

What did you say?

Which parts of your experience did he seem most interested in?

Which did he think were your weak points as far as the particular job at stake is concerned? Why did he think so? Did he feel there is some large or small prerequisite for this job which is missing from your background? If so, what was it?

Is there an important point you originally planned to introduce but didn't because the conversation got sidetracked or time ran out? Was there something of consequence you wish you had said but didn't think of until after you went out the door? There usually is.

Was there something you could have said better than you said it the first time around? Above all, what more did you learn about his problems, his needs?

When you sit down to write your letter, list these points.

Make your follow-up letter sell by demonstrating that you understand him and his organization. Most importantly, promise him something more, which you discovered or thought of since the interview, possibly something more which you have done in the interim to prove you're a better candidate. In other words, give him reason to believe that another interview will be well worth his time.

Include these seven points in your letter:

— Cite his pet subject—the one or two features of his organization or his way of doing things about which he seemed rather positively proud. Don't pour it on. Just mention it to show that you listened and remembered.

— Remind him of what he liked—the qualifications which he suggested he could use profitably.

— Recap the "Big Issue" from his point of view—that one major problem or question in his mind. If he was doubtful or critical, counteract, but don't let yourself slip into a defensive position. Express yourself positively. Emphasize some phase of your experience which will apply to his situation. Suggest that you know the answer and have the solution. Be specific, but don't go into too much detail. Whet his appetite so he'll want to see you to find out more.

— Use familiar language and names—the language he talks. Most executives have some favorite terminology of their own. Remember it and use some of it. If it is extreme or very unusual, put it in quotes so he'll know you're saluting him rather than stealing his stuff. And use the names of people who were referred to in the conversation or people whom you actually met. In other words, help him to visualize you as part of his organization.

— Indicate a readiness to produce—and while you're doing it, realize that there's a big difference between "readiness to produce" and "anxiety to get the job." The first is for the employer. The second is for you. Stick to the employer's perspective.

— Show enthusiasm—a genuine interest in him and his organization. It's always a selling point.

— Close with the next move in your control—that follow-up phone call. Tell him you will contact him next.

Here are three samples of follow-up letters used by applicants who got their jobs. Each of the authors represents a different field and different level of experience. But all of them employed precisely the same seven ingredients. The circumstances in each instance are as difficult as anything you will face, in fact, considerably more difficult than you will ordinarily experience.

Glance through all three of these letters first to familiarize yourself with the keynote, the something more, the plan, the idea, the suggestion, the sample of the applicant's ability to perform. Then if there's any question about the seven detailed points, check them over in the itemized lists following each letter.

A MID-CAREER EXECUTIVE FACES AN INTERVIEW FIRING SQUAD
AND STRIKES BACK TO WIN THE JOB WITH
THIS FOLLOW-UP LETTER

All went very well in the first hour of the initial interview between this applicant and his prospect, the president of a small manufacturing company. Then, the president looked at his watch and rang for three department chiefs. This was the first time he had ever mentioned his proposed purchasing department idea to his subordinates. In the remaining five minutes, the newcomers raised all kinds of objections. Then the president rushed off to another meeting, leaving the applicant in the awkward position of having to moderate a family argument.

Obviously, the key objection rested in the fact that the department heads did not want to relinquish their purchasing powers. Our friend was able, to some extent, to combat this by showing the potential time and money-saving advantages to each man involved. But time ran out with nothing resolved. And the applicant carefully planned this follow-up letter to help resolve the situation in his own favor.

Notice how the letter establishes this candidate as a specialist with a particular kind of experience which no other man in the organization could claim. Keep this approach in mind if you are being considered for a newly created position. Remember that in a situation like this, the employer usually needs an expert who knows more about some particular function than anybody in the existing organization. Emphasizing your "specialization" is your stock in trade as long as you don't talk in such a specialized way that the employer doesn't understand your language.

See how the letter tackles the main objection raised in the interview. The applicant reassures the boss that the new function can be created without upsetting the established organization.

284 West Bellevue Drive
Pasadena, Calif. 94309
213–476–4285

Mr. J. H. Stratton, President
Stratton & Morley, Inc.
Box 77
Culver City, Calif. 90230

Dear Mr. Stratton:

Our discussion last week left no doubt of your good reasons for establishing a central purchasing department. I would like the job of proving you are right. I know we could show results in six months, and still more at the end of the first year. And I am confident this can be accomplished without any plant interruptions or personal grievances on the part of department heads now purchasing their own capital items, materials, supplies, and customized requirements.

After our talk, I met with Mr. Gordon and Mr. Farnsworth and also Mr. Charbon. All of them seemed more receptive after I mentioned some of the helps and time savers which could be effected for their particular departments.

Since our meeting, I reviewed my own experience in helping to organize the first purchasing department for Holden and Company. Also, I queried some of my fellow purchasing agents at the NAPA convention last week especially regarding the delicate situation of removing purchasing controls from department heads.

I would like to discuss my findings with you and suggest a step-by-step plan to create your purchasing department. I can come to Culver City either at the beginning or end of next week. Which would be more convenient for you? I'll phone you this Friday morning to find out.

Very truly yours,

Arthur T. Wentworth

The seven points in this and the other sample letters are interwoven so that it isn't always possible to separate them. In some instances, one phrase, or one sentence, or one paragraph actually covers two or three points. But in case you've had difficulty identifying these key features, the following will guide you. See if you can find those sentences which accomplish two purposes.

His Pet Subject: ". . . your good reasons to establish a central purchasing department."

What He Liked: ". . . my own experience in helping to organize the first purchasing department for Holden and Co."

The Big Issue From His Point of View: ". . . this can be

accomplished without plant interruptions or personal grievances . . ."

". . . Mr. Gordon and Mr. Farnsworth and . . . Mr. Charbon . . . seemed more receptive after I mentioned some of the helps and time savers which could be effected for their particular departments."

Familiar Language and Names: ". . . capital items, materials, supplies, and customized requirements."

". . . Mr. Gordon . . . Mr. Farnsworth . . . Mr. Charbon."

Readiness to Produce: ". . . could show results in six months."

Enthusiasm: "I would like the job of proving you are right."

The Next Move in Your Control: "I'll phone you this Friday morning . . ."

A YOUNG DESIGN ENGINEER REKINDLES INTEREST WITH THIS
LETTER BY TRANSLATING HIS SELLING POINTS INTO
THE PROSPECT'S LANGUAGE

This young man's background consisted of seven years' design experience with a very large manufacturer. He had worked as one of fifty designers and was used to technical trade talk. He was applying for the job as the designer for a very small plant which had recently acquired a sub-contract for a government project.

The first interview resulted in not more than a hesitant maybe from his prospect. In reviewing the conversation a day later, the designer realized that his prospect was an administrator and a salesman, not an engineer. On second thought, some of the interview remarks indicated that the employer had only a layman's concept of the design problems in question.

In this follow-up letter the job hunter turns the tide by using his prospect's language and by pointing to what his particular experience could contribute to the job.

1271 Park Hill Drive
Cleveland Heights, Ohio 44118
216-267-3276

Mr. Clifford Otis, President
Judkins-Otis Manufacturing Co.
Box 207
Columbus, Ohio 43085

Dear Mr. Otis:

I want to thank you for my enjoyable visit to Columbus.

Your plant seems ideally arranged and the design work ahead sounds like a real challenge. It was a pleasure to meet Mr. Cox and Mr. Collins. I reiterate that I would very much like to contribute my personal interest and practical experience to the Judkins-Otis team.

As we discussed, my understanding of government agency engineers and their individual ways of doing things is essential to the job. I believe it was suggested that my knowledge of government specifications and regulations and forms is basic to the "routine procedure." That is true.

But there is a subtlety with respect to these details which is more significant than "routine." For example, of particular concern to you will be the fact that valve specifications with entirely different code numbers and names from one requisitioning agency to the next are in many cases actually verbatim copies. My familiarity with this one detail can represent a real time- and money-saver for you from the start.

I would like to meet with you again to illustrate exactly how this kind of thing can facilitate your expanded operation, especially when it becomes further involved in arrangements and rearrangements to meet government specifications.

Perhaps your next Cleveland visit would be a good time to confer. I will call your office Tuesday morning to learn where you can be reached and when it will be convenient for you to discuss this matter.

Yours truly,
Martin Stoner

Here are some of the seven ingredients identified. Look for more.

His Pet Subject: "Your plant seems ideally arranged . . ."

". . . the Judkins-Otis team."

What He Liked: "My understanding of government engineers . . ."

The Big Issue From His Point of View: "But there is a subtlety more significant than 'routine.' For example, of particular concern to you . . ."

Familiar Language and Names: ". . . arrangements and rearrangements . . ."

". . . Mr. Cox and Mr. Collins."

Readiness to Produce: "My familiarity . . . can represent time and money saved for you from the start."

Enthusiasm: "It was a pleasure to meet Mr. Cox and Mr. Collins."

". . . I would very much like to contribute my personal interest and practical experience . . ."

The Next Move in Your Control: . . . "I will call your office Tuesday morning . . ."

A HIGH-LEVEL EXECUTIVE COUNTERACTS INTERVIEW CRITICISM
AND SPEEDS HIS WAY TO A TOP POSITION
WITH THIS FOLLOW-UP LETTER

In an early interview, this man found himself unexpectedly surrounded at a luncheon conference by ten company officials who cross-examined him on details which he wasn't prepared to answer. He defended his general and vague answers by advising the group that he wanted to hear out each man before he came to premature conclusions. But this explanation drew a lukewarm reception. After two or three days to reflect on the questions, the applicant came back hard with specific answers in this letter.

Mr. George Aiken, President
Giant Advertising Agency
260 Madison Ave.
New York, New York 10016

Dear Mr. Aiken:

Thanks for a very pleasant and informative luncheon. I was pleased to meet all of your board members and principal department heads and to get a closer picture of their individual positions regarding the considered international advertising venture.

In the light of a later talk with George Stephens and several of your account supervisors, I have drawn up a plan which I believe is the most direct course to a productive international advertising program for Giant Advertising. My recommendation is an agency-integrated program virtually ready to go with only a small additional pilot staff and without any excessive new burdens upon your existing departments' functions.

The first of next week, I will telephone your office to learn when it will be convenient for you and your people to consider my detailed proposal.

Thank you for keeping this matter in confidence. You recall I am still employed.

Sincerely yours,
John DuBois

Roaring Brook Road
Chappaqua, New York 10514
914-218-6314

Review these seven points and look for more.

His Pet Subject: "... agency-integrated program ..."

What He Liked: "... with only small additional pilot staff and without any excessive new burdens upon your existing departments' functions."

The Big Issue From His Point of View: "... program virtually ready to go ..."

Familiar Language and Names: ". . . George Stephens and several of your account supervisors . . ."

Readiness to Produce: "... virtually ready to go ..."

Enthusiasm: ". . . pleased to meet your board . . . and . . . department heads..." "I have drawn up a plan..."

The Next Move in Your Control: "The first of next week, I will telephone your office . . ."

Your follow-up letter should not be more than one page. If there's more than that to say, get another interview to say it. Even if your letter contains only the best ingredients, if you make it longer than one page, you're probably elaborating so much that you kill the employer's motive to discuss the matter in person. Your one purpose is to get another hearing.

Remember too, that employers like job applicants who come to the point. Keep this in mind especially if you have a great deal of experience and are applying for an executive position where reducing things to their simplest form is a prime requisite of the job.

In average circumstances, it's usually a good idea to wait two or three days before mailing your letter. If you write the day after your meeting, you won't have time for the objectivity you need to plan your most effective strategy. Your letter might be nothing more than a repetition of what has just been said in the interview. What's more, if you wait a few days, until he's almost forgotten you, a letter serves the added purpose of reminding him to keep your application on top while he's interviewing others.

If you can casually learn from your prospect, or from his secretary, something about his up-coming activities, you will have the extra advantage of spotting a time when he isn't going to be so rushed and will give your letter the attention you want. If he's leaving the next day for an extended trip, hold your letter until one or two days after his return. If he's going to be involved in some special business for a specified time, wait one or two days after this involvement. But many employers will tell you they're extra busy all the time. In such a case, your only alternative is to dive right in. Mail your letter in two or three days.

There can be some circumstances when the two or three day rule doesn't apply. For one thing, if it is understood that there is some specific action you are going to take and then report back, don't relax in overconfidence. Speed may be your salvation. If the assignment is a challenging one, of course, it's important to do a good job. But remember, there are other applicants being interviewed for the same job, possibly every day. So each day counts.

If you've decided to carry out something more to reinforce your candidacy on your own, you might write your prospect in a day or so and tell him what you're doing. Specify when it will be ready for his consideration. Tell him you'll contact him at that precise time. But this procedure is only a stalling device. Get it done as fast as you can. Then write your letter. The stronger your follow-up letter, the greater the likelihood that your name will be on his calendar a second time.

CHAPTER XVI

How to Control Timing and Talk Salary

When to talk money.
The "asking price" trap.
Who has the key to the cash box?
The squeeze play.
When do you start?

What about money? We have already urged you to have your figures ready to match those which the employer has established for the job. Now you are concerned with "When should the subject normally be introduced?"

Ordinarily, the matter should not be discussed any sooner than toward the end of the first interview. If the employer starts talking money earlier than this, he may be either too shortsighted or too budget-strapped to consider the full potential of your qualifications. At the same time, he should usually be ready to mention some figures not later than the second interview. If he won't yield to any discussion of specific amount by this time, he's stalling for reasons which he will not or can not explain. His silence is a pretty sure sign he's not ready to do business with you.

You've laid your cards on the table, and it's his fair turn to show his hand. In a polite but firm way, you must make it clear that you expect this very soon, if not now. Don't allow yourself to shy away. Remember, the man who's interviewing you was probably looking for a job once. He's where he is today partly because he made some demands. He'll respect you if you do the same.

But if all goes well, he'll probably bring the subject up at the appropriate time. Wait for him until deadline time.

Your next concern is, how will he introduce the matter? Of course he may simply state that the salary is a certain amount and ask if that is satisfactory. Or he may try to force your hand and get you to volunteer the first figure. If you're lucky he will simply ask, "What's your salary request?" or "How much money do you want?" But he could put just a little twist on that last one and change it to, "How much money are you asking?" which implies that you'll settle for less. The catch questions and little tricks are numerous. There are a hundred and one ways of phrasing it so as to ease you into a defensive corner.

One of the difficult questions is, "How much are making now?" or "How much did you make on your last job?"

Perhaps you rightfully feel that your present or last salary has not been a fair return for what you contributed. Or you know for a fact that your pay has been below the going price for a person with your qualifications and in your field. You want and can get more money now.

In this case, the amount which you have been making is not the issue at all. Make it clear to your prospect before he gets the idea he can use your last salary as a frame of reference in dealing with you. However, if your interviewer insists upon approaching the money business from your old level, you might remind him politely that if you felt you were overpaid in your last or present job, you wouldn't be looking for a new one. He knows that perfectly well. But it might serve a tease purpose to remind him of it.

You might express your complete answer something like this:

"Mr. Employer, I'm ready for a new job because I'm well prepared to contribute more and earn more. One reason I'm equipped to earn more is because I've searched the market for the organization which could make the most profitable use of my particular experience. My special interest in you and your organization has been based in part upon good reasons to suspect that my background is especially adaptable to your problems and needs. And I think you'll agree that our conversation today verifies this." Continue by citing the specific functions you have discussed. Emphasize the particular experience and attributes which he has already admitted he could use profitably.

Finish something like this:

"As you know, I've had substantial experience in all of these areas. You are buying the best of it. And the best I can offer you now is worth more to you than something short of my best was worth to my last (or present) employer."

However your prospect introduces the subject of money, and whatever way you word the answer, your most effective approach is to point out that you're prepared to "contribute" more and hence to "earn" more. Follow it up with specific illustrations he's already admitted or implied that he likes and can use.

Does the individual who's interviewing you actually have the final authority to hire you, to establish the amount you are to receive and to effect payment? And, is the money there? You can't assume that these vital details are in perfect order regardless of how things appear on the surface. There's been many a slip in this area. The vast majority of employers are honest but interviewers representing well-established and highly reputable organizations have been known to misunderstand or misrepresent their authority. They promise or suggest a specified arrangement only to have their decision reversed by an official with higher authority. And you're even more likely to run into final arrangement difficulties with smaller, lesser known organizations.

At times it's a good idea to check the credit rating of your prospect. But good credit is not necessarily the answer to your problem at the moment. A corporation could be rated in the millions. But if there isn't a specified appropriation for the particular job you're discussing, you could be wasting valuable time. In plain logic, there is no job for you until, if ever, there's room in the budget.

Be especially mindful of possible misunderstanding if you are

applying to a new organization or in a newly created position
with an established employer. If you have some reason to suspect
something might not be in order, it's fair play by the end of the
second interview to find out who has the key to the payroll box.
You have every right to know sooner or later. Don't make it too
late.

When do you start? "Sometime in the near future" is obviously
not good enough. But neither is "in a couple of weeks" or "next
month". Not withstanding the resolve of all the other important
details, you don't have a job until you have a specified exact
starting date like nine o'clock, Monday morning, January 23rd.

As simple as this matter may seem, don't overlook it. This is
another area in which there's been many a slip either because the
candidate failed to pin down the employer or because the applicant wasn't sure when he'd be available.

You might get caught in a squeeze play between two different
employers at once. This can be tricky business. You could lose
both jobs if you're not careful.

First of all, never inform one prospective employer of your
dealing with another unless you are absolutely forced to do so.
In fact, don't even mention to one interviewer that you are
applying elsewhere. He knows that you're probably doing this.
But it won't do you any good to rub it in.

If by some unlikely chance you are asked, "Where else are you
looking? How do you stand with them?", consider the source
of the question. The inexperienced interviewer might possibly
have made inquiry because he doesn't trust his own opinion and
wants to find what others think of you. The experienced
interviewer might have planted this question to see if you will
boast unduly about how much in demand you are. In either event,
make light and brief of your answer and go on to the next subject.

If you do actually find yourself in a showdown between two
employers, you may have to face both of them with the facts. Be
honest and accurate if you don't want to get your signals crossed.
Supposing that a first employer has made you an offer on

Tuesday and wants your decision right away. Let's say you explain that you're very much interested but that you did previously promise another employer you'd see him on Wednesday, and frankly, you feel that you owe it to him and to yourself to keep the appointment with good intentions.

The first employer will probably appreciate your honesty and most likely hold his job for you until Wednesday afternoon or Thursday. Then on Wednesday you proceed as arranged to talk with the second company. They like you too. And the job looks a shade more desirable than the first one. But the second employer doesn't make a definite final offer.

Your only alternative now is to advise the later employer that you decidedly want to work for him but that another employer has made a definite offer which you agreed to settle one way or another by tomorrow. Maybe you can force the second employer's hand this way.

This is an awkward situation and a serious challenge. You have to make a decision on the spot, stick to it and be completely aboveboard with both parties. Never fabricate a predicament like this and try to force a hand. Such a scheme is almost sure-fire trouble. When you try to persuade one employer in this manner, it can be something like threatening Sally that she had better marry you today or else you'll marry Helen tomorrow. That would probably be the last you'd ever see of Sally if she amounts to anything. Employers are quite like humans in this respect.

You might try to establish the date as early as your first interview. Ask him, "Approximately when do you plan to move ahead with this matter?" Right then and there you should get at least an approximation. And the employer's reply, even at this stage, will be an indication of how seriously he's considering you and the job at stake. Needle him gently about this again in the second interview. You should get the exact answer by this time. If you don't get his committment by the third interview, something's probably wrong.

Be leery of the prospective employer who seems to linger, no matter how logical his reasons may sound. If he stalls very long, you may have to face the following probabilities. He may not be able to make up his mind about what he wants. This is a serious problem. But it is his problem. Don't let him make it yours by keeping you waiting. Or he may say he's pretty sure you're his man but he wants to interview others just to double check. There are employers who interview and interview while you wait for confirmation. Then they call you back for more talk. Then they interview others again. Finally they write you an apology saying, "Let's call the whole thing off." Or your prospect may be one who's hanging on to you just in case another preferred candidate won't take the job. But it's the preferred applicant who usually gets the job. And you can't afford to hold still at second place in any prospective employer's waiting line. There's another employer who wants you as his first choice.

Many of our Job Finding Forum people have strung along with one or another prospective employer for weeks in a situation which looks very promising only to find that the longer the wait, the less likely the marriage. Then one day, the applicant knocks on a new door which opens to love at first sight. He goes to work the following Monday morning. And employee and employer live prosperously ever after.

The law of averages for almost a quarter of a century of our Job Finding Forum practice promises the same reward for you. Just adhere to some objective self-appraisal. Keep at that job research, and you're certain to find the door with your name on it.

CHAPTER XVII

Sample Résumés

THE model résumés in this appendix are actual job-winning ones. They have been fictionalized to an extent. Names and certain identifying facts have been altered to insure privacy. In some instances the employer and clients are referred to in a general descriptive manner rather than by name. This is only for purposes of disguise. When you write your own résumé you must identify some of your employers exactly by name.

When you first look over these résumés you may feel that you can't describe your particular experience this way or point to such specific results. With due respect to these candidates, they were average people like the rest of us. They too believed it was impossible to pinpoint their ability and make such strong claims.

A MIDWESTERN BUYER PLOTS A SURE
COURSE TO A BIG NEW YORK
DEPARTMENT STORE WITH THIS RESUME

THE experience of this not-so-young woman included fourteen years of Midwestern department store buying and one long-since-previous two-year fling in New York. The lure of the big city, and the need for making a major personal readjustment at this time, called for an aggressive job campaign to reach long-distance prospects. This résumé established entirely new contacts for the applicant and opened the door to a big New York department store job.

Although the applicant's principal experience and last job was in the Midwest, this forward-looking résumé directs itself to the New York prospect's situation. Observe how the first page gets right to the point in case by calling attention to the job hunter's knowledge of the European market and by using previous New York experience to exemplify an important functional heading.

Miss Dorothy Grace
1212 Center Street
Cleveland, Ohio
872-1415

BUYER — DESIGNER DRESSES —

NEW YORK AREA DEPARTMENT STORE

ANTICIPATING STYLE TRENDS

While on a spring buying trip in Italy for Halle Brothers' "Little Salon," I was impressed with the casual, easy-to-wear clothes of a young designer, then relatively unknown. With a few pattern alterations to fit the American female figure and some simplification, I believed the dresses would be sensational in the Cleveland market. The designer was not in a position nor was he willing to manufacture for a mass market. His artistic temperament rebelled at allowing his creations to be changed or copied by some "ignorant and unfeeling" foreigner.

Driven by the fear that some other major store would discover my new genius, I cabled Mr. G., a Seventh Avenue manufacturer whose garments were well cut and beautifully made, in the hope that he could suggest a solution to my problem. Through some intensive, rushed detective work I finally found Mr. G. in Europe. My enthusiasm for the project communicated itself to him and he flew to Rome. Between his knowledge of pattern and make and my persuasion that the American market was a short cut to fame, we were able to get the designer to agree on basic terms of a contract to sell in the "Little Salon" the divine clothes of the now famous Camillo Camberra.

SELECTING SALABLE MERCHANDISE

When I was hired as the buyer of Better Dresses for Jay Thorpe, New York, I faced the necessity of revitalizing a department that, as a result of the long serious illness of the former buyer, was overstocked with potential markdowns. I decided to take the markdowns at once in order to obtain "open to buy" money. After gaining the cooperation and approval of the merchandise manager, I worked out a plan for introducing new and exciting clothes from hitherto unused sources and upgrading the unit price.

In one instance through long-cultivated personal contacts I was able to obtain a popular, quality line whose management was selling to a competitor. As a result of the attractive fashions plus an increase in the average amount of the saleschecks, the department showed a gratifying 30% gain in volume after one year's operation under my management.

MAINTAINING A PROPERLY BALANCED INVENTORY

Recently the comptroller at Halle Brothers inaugurated a new unit control system. The new procedure aroused antagonism and complaints on the part of clericals and sales personnel. Missing and carelessly recorded ticket stubs resulted in completely inaccurate pictures of certain departmental operations. To prevent this happening in my department I took care to familiarize myself with the important details of the system. A conference with my salespeople and office force explaining the need for the control system and the importance of following the new procedures was rewarded with their complete cooperation. The records of our department were an asset in keeping "Best Sellers" in stock during season and preventing the reorder of potential markdowns resulting from too heavy stock in any one category. Markdowns in the department that season dropped from 25% to 18%.

TRAINING SALES PEOPLE

As assistant buyer in the Sports Dresses at Schuster's, Milwaukee, the unplanned absence of the buyer during the early fall season left me in charge. Since I had been in the department for less than two months, I was not familiar with the new merchandise arriving daily. With the approval of the merchandise manager I enlisted the aid of our major sources in obtaining information about the goods on order.

I persuaded two of our manufacturers to send salesmen to assist in briefing our sales force at early morning meetings. Information from other suppliers received by mail and telephone was also discussed at the training meetings. The value of my training effort was reflected in complimentary shopping reports and was credited by the buyer for "... getting the season off to a good start."

ADVERTISING

During my first six months at Halle Brothers my department was suffering from lack of advertising space in the local papers. The advertising department, however, insisted that our department was getting its fair share of the available lineage.

On my next trip to the New York market I explained my problem to our new sources, and as a result, attractive and profitable cooperative advertising arrangements were offered to the store. Under the new arrangements the department's advertising space was increased 30% for the spring season.

PERSONAL

University of Wisconsin, B.A., 1966—English major

SUDDENLY UNEMPLOYED DUE TO CORPORATE MERGER, AN OVER-FORTY EXECUTIVE ADVANCES TO HIS FIRST NEW JOB IN TWENTY YEARS WITH THIS CAREFULLY DETAILED RESUME

NOTICE how this man's accurate description of what he did and how well he did it distinguishes this application from the chronological outline type of résumé which simply lists duties and responsibilities. This job hunter does not impose guesswork upon his prospective employers. He states his case completely in two short pages and leaves no doubt of his ability to perform. Even more importantly, between the lines he demonstrates that he is resou.ceful and an alert observer without expressing his own opinion about his personal characteristics.

These are the extras which will place any résumé on top of the pile for first consideration.

Alan M. Horwath
74 Fairmont Road
South Bend, Indiana 46619
219–864–6101

COMPTROLLER

PLANNING AND COST CONTROL

As comptroller for a steel distributing company, during a period of rapid sales acceleration, I proposed and put into action a new system of budgeting and cost control. Even though sales increased 160% in a five-year period, and losses were turned into profits, close supervision of expenses was required to permit building up of the company's working capital. Under my supervision of expenses during this period the company was able to restore its credit standing with banks and the trade to normal, and eliminate costly financing by a factor.

RESEARCH

As part of my plan I introduced a budget based on a combination of the company's recent records and operating figures from an industry study used by commercial banks. I appealed to our local bank, and they obtained from their correspondent in Chicago a composite financial statement and profit and loss figures of seven steel distributors of similar size to our firm. Using this information in relation to our expanding sales I was able to present the board of directors with a realistic budget, which proved to be attainable with a sharp increase in profits.

The perusal of other distributors' financial reports revealed to me the potential profit of a supplementary product line of related materials and services, which would incur very little additional overhead. Adoption of this suggestion further increased our earnings about 10% and permitted us to provide better and cheaper service to some of our large customers, including contractors, trucking lines and manufacturers.

ACCOUNTING

The increases in sales and payroll compelled the company to modernize its accounting system, and this task was assigned to me. My use of a decimal numbering system of accounts and IBM punch card machines made our inventory and expense records more accurate and produced daily reports of our actual position. Cumbersome record keeping was eliminated and office man power in the comptroller's office was cut in half. The newly acquired IBM machines were also utilized in payroll and billing accounts receivable.

These improvements permitted efficient and continuous supervision of plant operations, substantially reducing factory overhead and administrative expenses in proportion to sales. As a matter of fact, the clerical payroll for the entire company was about the same after sales increased over two and one-half times.

AUDITS AND REPORTS

The system of audits and reports I inaugurated insured the accuracy and reliability of accounting transactions. Frequent reviews of the company's property and insurance records assured adequate protection of its assets. In one instance, revision of coverage on our inventory, which I negotiated with our insurance broker, reduced the premium 18%. My new accounting records reduced the time spent by outside accountants in conducting their audit procedures. This benefited us in keeping auditing fees down.

CASH FLOW

My new records took the guesswork out of our cash forecast reports, and enabled us to present to our bankers an accurate forecast of income and borrowing requirements for the ensuing two years. Largely on the basis of this projection, the banks restored lines of unsecured credit, larger than previously available. Furthermore, the board of directors was able to plan the resumption of dividends on the company's stock.

TAXES

Radical changes in our profit picture necessitated frequent consultation of tax manuals. The company's various tax reports were prepared under my supervision, and I reviewed them in consultation with our auditors and attorneys. I sat in on consultations with Internal Revenue Service supervisors, successfully defending my computations, and only minor adjustments were required.

INVENTORY CONTROL

The administration and control of 3,500 inventory items was greatly improved. By programing these records into the machine accounting system, information was recorded with a minimum of paper work. Information on age, identification evaluation and location was now quickly available at a central reference station. The system also served to identify specific purchase and sales transactions.

Turnover of inventory increased from 3.4 to 5.1 times a year. Current conditions and trends were easily spotted in keeping parts and finished items at desired levels. This was particularly important while new items were being added as the company expanded.

EDUCATION

BBA University of Illinois, 1952

PERSONAL

Married, three children
Member, American Management Association

A PUBLICITY WRITER DEFINES HIS
EXPERIENCE PRECISELY IN THIS RESUME

HERE is a good illustration of pointing to tangibles in a field often thought of as too intangible to measure exactly. Remember, if you have done some sort of creative work for any consequential length of time, your employer continued to pay you because he benefited from your efforts. How did he benefit? These are the things your prospects want to know. Do not simply itemize a long list of your credits. They won't distinguish you from average because your competitor for the same job probably has just as long a list. Pick a few samples that were particularly effective and describe them in vivid detail to show how they were productive.

Clark Evans
428 Raymond St.
Chevy Chase, Maryland 20015
301–422–6204

PUBLICITY DIRECTOR

I have four years of newspaper background and ten years' experience in organizing publicity and in writing and placing news tie-ins and features for a national committee for aid to a foreign country, for a government agency in Washington and for a commercial radio and television broadcasters trade association.

ORGANIZING CAMPAIGNS

As an example, I was hired as publicity director for a national committee for aid to a foreign country at a time when intense public interest in other nations and international issues made it especially difficult to secure coverage for our remote cause. I developed a publicity kit with instructions and traveled to major cities across the country training prominent local personalities of our chapters in publicity techniques. Working with a head-quarters staff composed of one relatively inexperienced writer and one enthusiastic secretary-assistant I supervised publication of a weekly newsletter, a steady flow of news tie-ins and features and a guide for local publicity chairmen. The releases were distributed directly to the local chairmen who served as our leg men in placing the material in newspapers and on local radio and TV programs. In cooperation with the chapters, we re-established a defunct speakers bureau and in three years booked about 76 prominent nationals for about five hundred speaking dates at universities, schools, clubs, civic groups and religious affiliated organizations.

In the three years, as indicated by our clipping service, the annual publicity coverage increased an estimated 75% over what it was when I started. The program served its intended subtle purposes in specified Washington political circles and according to the national chairman, we did ". . . a superb job of stimulating enthusiasm and activity in our local chapters everywhere."

WRITING

I have written publicity ranging from fast, daily output of news tie-ins to longer features. It is a fair guess that most of the metropolitan dailies in the country have carried my material. As a member of the public relations department for a key government agency I composed news and features from newly released declassified information. This copy was widely published. So was a series I wrote on "The Grown Up War Babies" for the national committee for aid to a foreign country. *The New York Times*, for example, has carried my stories frequently. The CBS TV network has used my material a dozen times and *Newsweek* and *Time* have run parts of my in-depth features on some occasions.

PRESS RELATIONS

My publicity experience has called for constant press relations activity. I have personally placed many of the longer features referred to previously. And I have also employed my press contacts and knowledge of how the press works to defend my employers' position. For instance, as a member of the publicity staff for a commercial radio and television broadcasters trade association, I served as the press contact through two years of an anti-trust suit against the association. The suit was launched at a time when Washington investigations of broadcasting practices were making headlines unfavorable to broadcasters generally. Our suit was a conspicuous first of its particular kind and involved some high government officials and other name personalities. Through my two years on the receiving end of hundreds of press probes, less than two dozen consequential stories slanted against my employers were returned by the clipping services. To counteract, I visited strategic news sources, familiarizing them with our side of the story. This way I planted numerous favorable stories, several of which received page one placement in papers like *The New York Times, Chicago Tribune and The St. Louis Post Dispatch*.

Several of the very large city dailies which carried this favorable material were publications which, in the beginning, had employed back-stairway inquiry methods to seek out story lines which would have been seriously detrimental to our cause.

PHOTOGRAPHY

Before I became publicity director for the national committee for aid to a foreign country, I spent three months in that country on speculation gathering photographs and scripting photo stories. *Parade* magazine ran a four-page spread of some of the pictures with my script and cut lines. Others of these photos were purchased by outlets such as Rand McNally, Socony Mobil photo library and Pan American Airways. For part of my time on the public relations staff of the government agency in Washington I worked on the so-called "policy" desk gathering and selecting photos according to War and State Department directives. This material was used on about twenty-five "missions" throughout the world.

NEWSPAPER BACKGROUND

My early experience includes three years as a reporter for the *St. Louis Post Dispatch.* For an additional year I served as acting city editor of a Moline newspaper. I directed and assigned a news staff of eighteen reporters and photographers, planned make-up of local pages, wrote headlines and made up page dummies.

EDUCATION

A.B., University of Missouri School of Journalism, 1961
New York Institute of Photography

PERSONAL

Age 36, married, two children

CONSTRUCTION ENGINEER WINS NEW JOB
AGAINST STIFF COMPETITION WITH
THE "EXTRAS" IN THIS RESUME

THIS engineer could have written a good chronological résumé because his schooling and employment would automatically suggest that he knows what he wants and that he has progressed steadily in the same line of work from the start. But this functional résumé illustrates the "extras" which helped him win a much sought-after job. Notice how this job hunter not only shows his talent for organizing and trouble-shooting and working under pressure, but also proves he can get along well with people, company brass, sub-contractors, union officials and clients.

It is also interesting to note that the experience this man gained in working out his résumé helped him to make an important career decision. When he first launched his campaign, he felt that after years with very large companies, he wanted to move to a smaller organization. But as he developed this résumé, function by function, he realized that the things he enjoyed and did well were actually to be found in a larger organization.

Donald R. Kenmore
7300 Boulevard East
North Bergen, New Jersey 07047
201–869–4016

MANAGER OF CONSTRUCTION AND ENGINEERING

I have twenty years' experience in the employ of three major construction companies, for whom I have supervised construction of ten industrial facilities ranging in size from a $600,000 plant to a complex $20,000,000 project.

SUPERVISING CONSTRUCTION

For example, on one assignment I was sent to Canada as my firm's sole representative to build a plant on a tight schedule in time for a client, a chemical company, to fulfill a commitment. I solicited bids, negotiated contracts, and supervised the construction. The start of the project involved some delicate client relations concerning our understanding of the planned capacity. I resolved our differences agreeably and effected changes which increased the plant's capacity 15%. When a jurisdictional union dispute threatened to tie up the job, I arranged talks with national leaders of unions concerned and obtained an agreement which averted work stoppage.

The plant was ready for start up two months ahead of schedule.

On another out-of-town project, to keep within a restrictive budget I gained authorization to negotiate sub-contracts and change orders. My changes and dealings with local contractors made it possible to hold costs of this 150,000-square-foot, steel construction multi-level garage under $11.00 per square foot. Extra work charges were under ¾ of 1% and the profit margin for my employer was about 15%.

COORDINATING TEAM WORK

On both small and large scale projects I have worked with the problems of coordination between mechanical design groups in my charge and other design groups and between design sections within my company and numerous sub-contracting engineering firms.

For example, in one instance, for an aluminum complex, I

coordinated the work of about 50 designers involving approximately 1,200 drawings and I supervised the combined efforts of purchasing agents and expediters. I approved plans, specifications, purchase orders and invoices of sub-contract engineers for the general facilities portion of this $300,000,000 project. I also coordinated the operations of mechanical and electrical suppliers.

On another occasion, at the time of a critical steel situation, a client requested an advance in schedule for the erection of a maintenance shop. I obtained authorization to purchase "warehouse" steel, found a source, and then coordinated the efforts of company and sub-contractor design groups to revamp the design in terms of the available steel. Through periodic visits I was able to project a better understanding of the problems and urgency in speeding up production. The steel was delivered to the job site one week ahead of schedule.

ENGINEERING

My engineering work has been primarily in the design of power and industrial plants and has involved equipment ranging from a simple thermometer to complex control systems, from an ordinary pump to large boilers and turbine-generators. For four years in the employ of a large construction firm operating in many countries, I served mostly as a heat balance specialist until, at the vice president's request, I trained five other engineers.

When I became involved in the aluminum plant project, a design philosophy had already been decided upon for both the maintenance and power facilities. I prepared an analysis to show that there were unnecessary duplications of equipment in the maintenance shop. I proposed an alternate plan which was adopted. Eight years later, this plant is operating efficiently at 110% of design capacity.

PURCHASING

My experience includes purchasing of equipment, materials and selection of subcontractors involving expenditures of a little over $4,000,000.

In one case, after separate bid evaluations had been made for a number of items and apparent low bidders had been tentatively selected, I noticed that one company was involved in more than one item. At my suggestion, a package deal was consummated and saved my employer $60,000.

On another occasion, one of five reputable bidders came in

unreasonably high, about 25%. At my instigation, this bidder
was called in for questioning, and it turned out that the quoted
price had inadvertently been for four rather than three units. The
apparent high bid thus became the low bid at a saving to my
company of about $30,000.

PLANNING AND EVALUATION

On virtually every assignment, I have been brought in on the
early stages of a project to help set up schedules, plan man-power
needs, establish work procedures and estimate costs.

On numerous occasions I have been delegated to make preliminary studies to determine relative merits of alternate solutions
considering items such as costs, revenue, possibilities of obso-
lescence and reliability of an installation. One such study was for
a utility company when only meager data was available. I had
to develop my own anticipated performance data from which I
analyzed plant investment costs, including periodic expansions,
operating costs and revenue for a period of 30 years. My analysis
was used to specify the size and operating conditions of the proposed plant. Completed about 10 years ago, this study set a pattern which is still being observed by the utility in its installations.

EDUCATION

M.E., Virginia Polytechnic Institute, 1943
Languages: Moderate command Spanish, French

PERSONAL

Age 40, married, four children

FORMER DRAMATIC DIRECTOR WITH ONLY TWO YEARS' FREE-LANCE COMMERCIAL EXPERIENCE PROJECTS INTANGIBLE QUALIFICATIONS IN THIS RESUME TO ADVANCE INTO A STEADY, GOOD PAY SALES JOB

HERE is a sample of a modified chronological-type résumé which uses the names of projects in order instead of functional headings. Notice, however, that the applicant has adhered to the problem-solution-results pattern in describing what she did. Dates of employment are not indicated in this résumé because each of the jobs was actually a short-term assignment and a listing of dates would suggest that the applicant was an unsteady, undecided job hopper.

One of the most important features of this résumé is what was left out of it. The job hunter does not mention several odd jobs which she held in between the positions itemized in the résumé. And she does not discuss her ten years as a college dramatic director. This extensive experience was, of course, important in her life. But it is not important to the prospective employer. What is more, elaboration on the artistic career would have defeated the purpose of portraying the applicant as a hard-sell real estate representative.

If your principal experience has been gained through self-employment or free lance work, keep in mind that some employers will shy away from you because they doubt that you could follow company policy direction and they suspect that your lone wolf experience doesn't qualify you for teamwork.

Study this résumé to see how careful the applicant has been in strategic spots to show her hand at work digging into company problems and working cooperatively for and with other people.

Mrs. Ellen Cavanaugh
16 East 92nd Street
New York, New York 10028
212–348–6693

SALES AGENT: LUXURY COOPERATIVES
(ON-THE-PREMISES)

116 EAST 64TH STREET

Five-room duplexes with northern exposure were one of my
major sales problems as agent for William A. White & Sons on
this project. Located in the center of the building, the apartments
received minimum light and their "picture" windows faced an
old brick wall and fire escapes. Clients balked when they discovered the view. Several prospects, sold on the plan and ready
to buy, took one look and walked out.

To counteract this sales resistance, I made on-the-hour tests to
determine light values and sun patterns in the apartments. I
found they actually received mellow, pleasing reflections from
the red brick wall—antique browns, blues, pinks, greens, yellows
and purples. At certain times of day the sun reflected these colors
and a rosy glow enveloped the suites, enhancing their decorative
potential. And the angular lines of the fire escapes made an ideal
subject for leisure time sketching.

I incorporated these new found features into a presentation
slanted toward a feminine appeal. With this different perspective,
female prospects took a second look and within six months, I sold
the nine remaining duplexes.

THE MANCHESTER

On twelve-hour notice, I picked up loose ends of an emergency
situation at The Manchester shortly after its sales office opened.

A prime location, architect Resnick's maximum use of minimum
space, building quality and craftsmanship and extensive advertising seemed to augur well. The sales office was busy but Douglas
Elliman, Gibbons & Ives was not attracting the desired clientele.

From my on-the-spot position, I recognized the difficulty was
due in part to the vague tenant image projected in our ads. The

Manchester was not sufficiently distinguished from nearby competitors. And the media were not reaching the right prospects.

My proposal to alter our advertising was adopted and I worked with the sales vice president and advertising agency to effect the changes. Despite a poor Wall Street market, we were able to attract and secure the desired tenants in less than a year.

REGENT HOUSE

Securing five-year leases at "unheard of" rentals during a period of recession was the challenge I faced when I joined Fisher Brothers' rental team for this project. With the bulk of less expensive apartments having been rented, I was assigned to secure the long leases for the most luxurious tower and large upper-floor suites.

To accomplish this, I created a publicity and sales promotion program featuring the building's well-known tenants, international publicity, its size and the fact that it was a "first of its kind" in New York. I indoctrinated public relations groups and supplied selected publications and columnists with a steady flow of news items associated with the name of the building. To seek out prospective tenants, I screened hundreds of telephone inquiries resulting from the publicity.

In six months, I secured eight major deals.

THE SHONNARD

When The Shonnard, 100% cooperative with hotel services, opened its recent advertising campaign, I was called in to handle sales and negotiate long and short term rentals in the absence of the building's assistant manager. Inasmuch as The Shonnard prides itself on having its cake and eating it too, it was difficult to enter an occupied apartment for showing and often necessary to sell "plans" and "sample" apartments.

Working against this handicap, I sold four co-ops and secured 10 rentals despite a 20% increase in rent over the previous year.

PERSONAL

Widow.

Sales lecturer. Toured schools and colleges such as Vassar and Bryn Mawr. Currently, Saturday lecturer, The Barbizon School of Fashion Merchandizing.

Assistant to the president, House Syndicate Corp.

EDUCATION

B.A., Milligan College; M.A. in Theatre-Speech, University of Virginia, 1955.

A MID-CAREER ADVERTISING AGENCY
ACCOUNT EXECUTIVE PINPOINTS HER
NEW JOB TARGET IN THIS RESUME

IN a thorough investigation of her possible job prospects this applicant employed trade publications, trade associations, directories of advertisers and advertising agencies, advertisers' annual reports, and two banks. She also sought out further critical information from members of her luncheon club and college alumnae association. She even acquired some useful detailed facts from the switchboard operators of her prospective employers.

This résumé is directed to one single prospect who was discovered to be interested in landing an armed forces recruiting account and who listed among its existing clients a glassware manufacturer and a chemical and drug manufacturer, both soon up for renewal.

Read this sample and observe how it adheres strictly to selected examples of the applicant's experience as applied to one specified prospect.

In her alternate résumés, this job hunter used the same functions with some different examples selected according to the other prospects' particular interests.

No matter how many prospects you wish to cover in your job campaign, an excellent way to learn how to write an effective résumé is to select one specified prospect and practice directing a résumé toward a realistic situation as it actually exists.

Martha J. Secor
14 Wood Hill Drive
Mount Kisco, New York 10549
914-666-1874

ACCOUNT EXECUTIVE

In fourteen years with four advertising agencies I have worked in creative planning, client contact and the administration of accounts. For the last six years I have been an account executive with an agency which bills fifty million dollars.

SUPERVISING AND ADMINISTRATION

For instance, I have supervised and coordinated the efforts of all our agency departments to produce a program of magazine advertising, TV, radio, billboards, and numerous collateral merchandizing materials for an armed forces recruiting account.

Despite relatively modest billing, considerably more has been involved than usual, necessitating excessive client contact with many Washington officials, including the assistant secretary for the service. And our success has depended greatly on precise budget bids and required government production controls.

There has been no consequential error in execution of these details. The clients are enthusiastic about the improvement in their recruiting goals. Our three-year contract, which can be cancelled after any one year, has been recently renewed.

CREATIVE PLANNING
..... *To Overcome A Special Merchandising Problem*

Prior to the first summer after we had established a new glass baking dish line for our glass manufacturer client, the general sales manager came to us charging that it was impossible to overcome the jobber's decision to drop the line for summertime promotion and display. In a rush job using mostly print media, we created a campaign showing that fruit pies and casseroles are baked in summertime, that iced tea and coffee have to be brewed, and that both cooking and clean-up time are reduced when our product line is usd. This campaign, slanted toward both customer and distributor, turned the tide of jobber acceptance. Within one month from the time this material was placed in effect, distribution increased and summer sales went up beyond the wintertime level.

..... *To Create A New Market For An Old Product*

When our client, a leading drug manufacturer, faced the problem of how to interest bottlers in vitamin fortification of beverages, I proposed we invent a mythical bottler in the form of a caricature and develop an advertising and sales promotion program around him right down to bottle labels featuring the Vitamin C "health bonus." We produced complete advertising kits for bottlers and appeared at bottling conventions and sales meetings with displays centered around a life-size, three-dimensional figure of our "character." The client soon gained a dozen important customers with the help of this promotion. At the same time, my activity in the bottling industry to service this account formed the missionary work which was primarily responsible for my agency's gaining one of the major soft drink bottlers as a new account.

MARKETING COUNSEL

For example, a chemical manufacturing client proposed to follow a competitor and spend a million dollars to promote antibiotic treatments for delaying spoilage of poultry products. I coordinated the efforts of our market research people in a study of poultry processing and shipping and pricing factors and distribution patterns. We determined that spoilage of poultry was not a significant problem for retailers and consumers. Furthermore, processors and shippers would probably abuse the extra days before spoilage by distributing farther. This research saved our client a great deal of money while the competitor had moved too fast on insubstantial market information and faulty assumption.

DEVELOPING NEW BUSINESS

I have worked with agency teams to prepare and make presentations to gain approximately ten million dollars of new accounts over the last seven years. For example, in soliciting the previously mentioned recruiting account, I supervised an extensive field investigation of recorded interviews with recruiters and other service personnel on the job at military installations across the country. Competing against four other agencies, we won this two-million-dollar account with presention of this grass-roots material.

A twenty-minute film I conceived on how advertising supports the recruiters was largely responsible for our renewing this account. The client later used prints of this film for training new recruiters.

EDUCATION

A.B., U.C.L.A.; M.B.A., Harvard—Business Administration

PERSONAL

Married, two children

Guest Lecturer on Advertising four years, New York University

A MID-CAREER PURCHASING AGENT UNEMPLOYED EIGHTEEN MONTHS FOUND A HIGHLY REWARDING NEW JOB WITH THIS RESUME

THIS applicant used an introductory "scope" statement in his résumé because he knew exactly what his prospects needed and could summarize his qualifications precisely to those specifications. The problems, solutions, results are indicated very clearly in each function. Can you spot them? From his research, this job hunter learned that his prospects were concerned importantly with the cooperative relationship between the purchasing department and other departments. It was certain that the ability to get along well with people would be a key qualification. Notice how this winning candidate used words like "we" and "our" and "us" and other factual phrases and sentences to prove he was considerate of fellow workers.

George Harpen
97 King Ave.
Weehawken, N.J. 07087
201–865–9463

DIRECTOR OF PURCHASING

Over a period of sixteen years for the Aiken Company and for J. M. Maserick, Inc., I have organized and directed purchasing. In each case, beginning with loose ends of a decentralized procedure I have established an integrated department to bring about savings of approximately a $150,000 annual average for these small manufacturers.

REDUCING COSTS

For instance, when I was assigned to organize purchasing for Maserick, I found that steel reinforcing bars were being purchased from a major mill in stock lengths at standard prices. I located a smaller local mill which could shear small lots to required lengths. This mill further agreed to furnish new rolls for a more efficient section, and to use billets to yield bars having a higher tensile strength. Lead time was cut from thirty to fifteen days. With reduced waste and shearing costs annual savings exceeded $35,000.

In another situation, I discovered that a competitor was obtaining wood fiber to similar specifications as ours from the same source at a lower price. The suppliers exercised firm price control in view of geographic limitations for its manufacture and marketing. I found a new supplier geographically non-competitive and negotiated a price for material to our specifications 13% under our current rate. In turn we were able to arrange that same new price with the original supplier who was retained for reasons of convenience to us. A competitive advantage for this component was gained with an annual savings of $25,000.

ANALYZING COSTS

I initiated cost and value analyses to determine whether to "make or buy." The customized items most frequently involved steel fabrication, metal stamping, wire-forming and woodworking. Gaining the cooperation of other departments which had previously preferred to do their own purchasing, I frequently found savings to 50% in having steel manufactured by steel fabricators instead of by our own forces and by farming out certain maintenance operations.

PLANNING AND FORECASTING

For example, in one instance steel order schedules were being projected for three- and four-month periods via meetings of sales and production heads ascertaining requirements from the data of the moment. This procedure brought about irregular and heavy inventories, frequent cancellations and sometimes complete depletion of an item. I devised a graphical system correlating sales quantities with production units. Plotting took but a few minutes weekly. The information was always current and obviated time-consuming meetings. My system made possible the maintenance of safe minimum inventories, eliminated work stoppages and reduced cancellations by 90%.

DEVELOPING SYSTEMS & ADMINISTRATIVE PROCEDURES

I have developed administrative procedures to improve controls and to save time and money.

For instance, for Aiken Manufacturing, I installed a visible posted record system for all items purchased repetitively. Savings resulted from discount quantity ordering. Supplier prices were more easily controlled. Inventory errors were more readily spotted. Price information for other departments, formerly obtainable only with time-consuming difficulty, became easily accessible.

On another occasion, when excessive correspondence in comparing bids was causing consequential delays, I installed a standard business form system for quotation requests on capital items, materials, supplies and customized requirements. I prepared specifications and directed bid analyses in cooperation with each interested department. This reduced correspondence 50% and improved day-to-day working relations between purchasing and other departments.

EDUCATION

B.S., Worcester Polytechnic Institute, 1960.

PERSONAL

Married, two children. Member N A P A.

USNR Lieutenant—World War II Engineering Liaison, French Carrier

AFTER A NINE-YEAR ABSENCE TO START A FAMILY, THIS NOT SO YOUNG MOTHER RETURNS TO THE WORKING WORLD AND A BETTER POSITION THAN HER PREVIOUS JOBS WITH THIS RESUME

AN important rule in writing a résumé after prolonged absence from work is to de-emphasize details which might make your experience sound like ancient history. This applicant has avoided dates and other specifics which would be associated with yesteryear. For example, the names of two principal employers were omitted in the original résumé from which this sample was taken because those employers merged with a second firm so that the company name is different now.

The omission of names is a serious void in a résumé and necessitates an extra effort to prove your worth. But it can be done. Notice how this applicant concentrates on leaving no questions about her ability to perform, especially when she specifies tangible, proof-positive results in areas where results are often thought of as being intangible and indescribable.

Attention is called to the omission of basic secretarial skills in this résumé. In this case, the applicant did have a wealth of administrative experience and was applying for a higher level job which called for decision making and relieving the boss of administration above the level of routine detail. Mention of dictation and typing speed would automatically anti-climax the more important functions and claims.

But be cautioned that this does not apply to a job hunter with lesser secretarial experience, where specifying speeds at basic secretarial skills is a must.

Joan Simmons Thomas
3 Garret Place
Bronxville, New York 10708
914–337–7409

EXECUTIVE SECRETARY

(TO VICE PRESIDENT ADVERTISING, SALES PROMOTION)

EXECUTING ADMINISTRATIVE DETAILS

For example, when the vice president of a nationally known Radio-TV station representative firm was suddenly called out of town on an unexpected business trip, as his secretary I set up the next year's advertising budget as he had directed hurriedly from scratch paper notes, assorted memos, and some sections from the previous year's budget, comparing budget estimates and actual expenses and showing net changes. My final compilation of this material was ready upon his return. It was presented to the president and the board exactly as I had prepared it.

In another instance, to help evaluate and set up a system for reducing and controlling communications expenses, I made a comparative cost study of the salesmen's use of teletype, telephone and telegraph as well as a survey of all telephone equipment used in the organization. My study formed the basis for revised procedures and changes in equipment which the company comptroller said "... represented consequential savings in our communications costs."

ORGANIZING

To assist the sales promotion department in improving selling aids for salesmen, I analyzed needs of radio program information files by checking against current station schedules. I wrote or spoke directly to stations' managers to gain their cooperation in obtaining up-to-date material. I edited or abstracted this material according to sales slant, type of program, rate and schedule data. I advised all our branch offices of changes. A few months after I completed this work, the manager told me, "There was a one hundred per cent improvement in these files. They have proved to be much more useful selling tools."

I screened, selected and organized new information from newspapers, trade and business publications for possible new business opportunities, and for reference in preparing presentations, speeches and planning business programs and campaigns. This material was in continual use not only by my immediate superior but also by at least a dozen other company executives.

CORRESPONDENCE

My work has usually included fairly heavy correspondence. For example, as secretary to an account supervisor in a large advertising agency, I composed many communications under his direction and answered others on my own according to his policies as I understood them. About 50% of his correspondence for three years was written by me without his having to review it at all. When he was out of town on extended business trips, I screened his correspondence and prepared a daily digest of it for his attention when he phoned in. In the vast majority of instances, I wrote letters of reply based upon his brief telephone instructions which often ended with his remarking, "You know what I want to say."

ADMINISTERING LEGAL AND FINANCIAL DETAILS

For one other employer, the corporate secretary of a large architectural firm, I forwarded invitations to bid to selected contractors, confirmed their acceptance, and organized distribution of drawings, specifications and proposals received so that they were ready for meeting on specified dates. After the contracts were awarded, I followed through on details relative to preparation, transmittal and signing of contracts.

When the vice president of a large New York bank, which was one of my company's clients, suddenly called my employer for a quick report on costs to date on their new bank building being constructed, in twenty-four hours I completed an outline of all costs to date including supplementary orders. This report was used by my employer in making his reply and left in the hands of the client just as I composed it.

ADMINISTERING CONFIDENTIAL & PERSONAL MATTERS

Each of my three employers eventually entrusted me to keep records of personal matters, expense accounts, income tax details and investments as well as confidential company figures and statements.

SUPERVISING PERSONNEL

On several occasions, I have hired, trained and supervised clerical personnel. For instance, when one employer assigned me to work out a special and very long report in ten days' time, I organized and assigned work to three company pool typists and borrowed a proofreader from another department. This job was completed ahead of time. Two of the pool typists and the proofreader requested permanent assignment to my office despite the extra hours and pressure placed on them in this rush job.

EDUCATION

A.B. degree, Brown University, Providence, R.I.
School of Business Administration, Pace University
New York University—special course: Review course for
Secretaries
Investments & Securities
Personnel Management
Advertising & Selling

PERSONAL

Married
Secretary, Brown University Club of New York

A TOP-LEVEL EXECUTIVE REDUCES A WEALTH OF APPLICABLE EXPERIENCE TO ITS SIMPLEST FORM IN THE TWO PAGES OF THIS RESUME

NOTICE how this applicant does not anywhere indicate his total years of experience and makes only casual reference to years in just two of the functions. Instead he places emphasis on what he did and indicates scope and depth with specific figures like, ". . . staff of three thousand in fifty-nine countries," ". . . billing has grown more than one thousand per cent. . ." and ". . . sales increased from eighteen million dollars to one hundred eleven million dollars . . ."

Remember, if you have substantial experience, do not attempt to rest your whole case on the amount of time you've spent at it. Be certain you point to more meaningful measures of breadth and depth and specify results.

You will see that, contrary to our general rule, this high level executive does editorialize and express his opinion on his subject. In applying for a top level position, you can sometimes be expected to have a knowledge which your prospective employers do not possess. In such a case, don't hesitate to give them a little taste of your opinion regarding your specialty. Just be very careful not to mention the obvious which would insult the employers' intelligence. And keep it brief so they'll want to see you in person to find out more.

Bjorn Dressler
27 Hobart Ave.
Short Hills, New Jersey 07078
201–747–7234

DIRECTOR,

INTERNATIONAL ADVERTISING & MARKETING

ADMINISTRATION

As director of the international division of a 4 A advertising agency, I have developed and supervised the international advertising of a leading U.S. chemical company, a major electronics equipment manufacturer, a division of an oil company and three food products clients. Some of these have their domestic advertising with other agencies.

Over the last seven years, I have organized our international division so that it can function either autonomously or as an integral part of other agency branches, depending upon the particular client's needs and the agency's economy in each case.

While virtually all of the client contact for international accounts is conducted by my own staff, five other agency departments contribute to the advertising programs of some of our international accounts. Other clients are serviced exclusively by our international staff of specialists in media, creative work, production and traffic. I hired the key personnel and oriented them in policy matters. The overseas work is effected through a network of affiliated agencies which I selected and which represent a total staff of three thousand people in fifty-nine countries.

My previous experience in administration of international advertising includes four years with another large chemical company for whom I established the international advertising department and directed advertising in five continents.

ACCOUNT CONTROL

I have also organized my present division so that accounts can be controlled either through our centralized operation or through decentralization, depending upon the nature of the marketing task and the size of the client's overseas staff. This flexibility has proven a result-getting new business tool and the key to our securing one very large consumer account and several other consequential new clients.

At the same time, I have placed considerable emphasis on minimizing our decentralization which, in my opinion, is the greatest single weakness in international advertising. More and more American advertisers are questioning the effectiveness of decentralization and seeking advertising facilities which will give their headquarters office a world-wide advertising and marketing concept.

MARKETING

I work closely with our clients and our account executives to determine marketing strategy. Sometimes this results in our becoming more than marketing counselors. On several occasions we have developed special marketing projects paid for by our clients. For instance, three of our account executives were dispatched to different parts of the world to study the dairy industry and one client's market potential. As a result, this client's billing with us has grown more than one thousand per cent in two years and they are still expanding their international advertising and marketing efforts.

Recently we have employed visual presentations of our market analysis to convince top management of advertisers that retailing abroad is undergoing a revolution. For example, with the trend overseas toward self-service and supermarkets being little understood, I personally traveled to major European markets to capture this activity on film. Demonstration of this one film resulted in substantially increased budgets for my division and consequential alteration in marketing strategy and distribution methods of our international advertising clients. As a public service promotion for my agency, I have created and published a bi-monthly marketing information bulletin for U.S. companies involved with consumer products retailing abroad. This bulletin is now distributed to four hundred executives at their written request.

CREATIVE PLANNING & PRODUCTION

Except in the case of highly technical products, a major share of my departmnt's world-wide advertising is based upon creative platforms developed here and adapted abroad. The media strategy and production methods are supervised by specialists to minimize production difficulties inherent in international advertising and to offset hazards of decentralization. This practice has won my agency a number of citations. For example, we just received the highest award in international advertising. Three of our corporate ads are being cited by the Swiss advertising art publication, *Graphis Annual,* which each year selects the best advertising from each country whether for local or international use.

BACKGROUND

My background includes three years as Export Sales Manager for a division of a large chemical corporation. By developing new markets and imparting flexibility into what had been a rigid, passive sales organization, we increased sales from eighteen million dollars to one hundred eleven million dollars during my tenure.

EDUCATION

Bachelor's Degree—Sorbonne University, Paris
Advanced Courses—Penn State—International Law
Columbia—Political Science

PERSONAL

Born in Switzerland, Age 42.
Lived in France, Germany, Switzerland, Holland, Belgium
Languages—French, German, some Spanish
Married, three children

MEMBERSHIPS

International Advertising Association, International Committee of the 4 A, American Marketing Assocation.

AN ENTERPRISING YOUNG SALESMAN DESCRIBES HIS EXPERIENCE IN HIS OWN STRAIGHTFORWARD LANGUAGE TO DISTINGUISH HIMSELF AS ABOVE AVERAGE IN THIS RESUME

EXAMINE this résumé to see how effectively the job hunter shows his hand at work in solving the problems he faced. Notice how, in his own plain language, he talks about the little extras in his performance. Without them, this résumé would have portrayed the applicant as just another salesman carrying out routine duties. Whatever your job level may be, this is a simple example of how much more forceful you can be by actually describing how you do things rather than just assuming that the employer understands what you did.

Read this résumé a second time and you'll probably feel that you are out there on the firing line with this man making calls and closing sales. This is the kind of lively demonstration which gains the prospective employer's confidence.

John R. Grosvenor
65 Sheridan Ave.
Mt. Vernon, New York 10552
914–668–9731

SALES REPRESENTATIVE –

TOILETRIES MANUFACTURER

DEVELOPING A TERRITORY

For a beauty product manufacturer, I was selected to improve sales of an item which had been moving slowly in upper Manhattan and the Bronx. When I took over, the wholesale sales volume for this product in this market was less than $20,000 annually. The product was advertised only four times yearly in one consumer magazine. In reviewing the situation, I concluded the job called primarily for intensive, fast moving coverage which necessitated creating a system to utilize my time at maximum efficiency.

I organized my calls into groups of twelve or fifteen, each group to represent an area, or a day's work. I secured maps of the boroughs and cut out the sections to be covered. I drew a smaller map of each area within the sections to paste on the lead sheet of an area. These smaller maps showed starting points, street direction and parking places. On each call sheet I recorded purchases, displays installed, buyer's hours, name and address.

This system enabled me to see every neighborhood drugstore in my territory every sixty days. In fourteen months I increased the sales volume to $60,000.

INTRODUCING A NEW PRODUCT

For example, I was charged with the responsibility of introducing a new product in Detroit. I worked out my own sales promotion program and secured full cooperation of dealers in using this plan although they had never tried such a method before.

I sold two leading beauty supply houses 144 deals of hair set and made a date to meet with their sales staff. One week later we started the promotion by presenting the selling aids and sales plan to the sales people, and I spent two days in the field with each one. Twenty selling days later, 102 deals or about 1,500 single units had been sold.

CUSTOMER RELATIONS—MARKET KNOWLEDGE

While calling on beauty salons in Michigan, I met a salon owner who liked our product but wasn't obtaining the best results possible using it. As an experiment, I volunteered to make a demonstration on a customer and had the salon owner and two operators participate. The operators were sold. So was the owner who placed a new order twice the size of any of his previous orders.

This paved the way for my plan to cover all of the central states with minimum time in each territory by concentrating on spotting dealers who would promote my line for me. I gained authorization from my company to pay a fee to dealers who would use their salons for demonstration and provide the products. The dealers' response to this proposal was usually favorable and I was able to pick and choose on a pretty selective basis.

Seventy-five per cent of these deals improved sales in specified territories. As one example, a dealer in Grand Rapids did $10,000 in sales of our line that year as against his previous average of about $3,200 annually.

EDUCATION

School of Business Administration, Wayne (State) University, Detroit

PERSONAL

Age 28, married, two children

TOP LEVEL SPECIALIST CREATES A NEW JOB
FOR HIMSELF USING THIS RESUME
AS HIS MAJOR SELLING TOOL

RESTRAINED in his old job for years by big company politics, office personality clashes and an unappreciative top management, John Cornell applied his talent for research to his own personal problem and came up with several new prospects who could benefit from his specialized experience.

This résumé is a good example of describing former experience in terms of the prospects' present interests. It projects into the future rather than rehashing the past. The problems and specific examples mirror the prospects' needs exactly. Beyond that, the functional headings for this high level position are designed to call attention to methods and skills which the prospect may not have previously considered for all they could be worth to him.

Whatever your work or level of experience may be, remember that your résumé functional headings are only as good as they apply to your prospect's situation determined by job research. It's the forward-looking résumé that hits home for winning a job campaign.

John M. Cornell
Linden Road
Darien, Conn. 06820
203–327–4333

DIRECTOR, CORPORATE PURCHASING RESEARCH

I have fifteen years' diversified experience in commercial research and purchasing including eight years as director of purchasing research for a company with sales in excess of five hundred million dollars annually.

PROCUREMENT PLANNING

Directing Cost Reduction Efforts:

Cost improvements were being missed as purchasing efforts were concentrated on materials at the top of the dollar array. I introduced a new system to direct cost reduction projects into areas with the greatest profit impact. Within four months after my recommendations were applied, costs were reduced $95,000 per year on two chemicals which had been frozen on a cost plateau.

Planning for Negotiations:

I worked closely with corporate and division purchasing agents to insure that the right information was available when needed. For example, two months prior to contract negotiations for an important organic chemical used at ten plant locations, I pointed out that the already large requirements were scheduled to increase 40 per cent over the next five years. Economic studies completed under my supervision—plus detailed production cost estimates—resulted in a contract which reduced costs by over $200,000.

RESEARCH ON PURCHASED MATERIALS

Commodity Studies:

I have prepared over one hundred economic surveys on materials in a wide range of industries; recommendations from these surveys have resulted in improved buying. For example, in one such study on adhesives, made at the request of the division purchasing agent, I recommended that we commit for six months' usage at a firm price; a saving of $25,000 resulted.

Commercial development asked our purchasing research group to make a worldwide supply and demand analysis of steroid hormone. This imported raw material was in critically short supply and, as a result, we were considering manufacturing the product. My report pointed out that, contrary to trade opinion, world supplies would be plentiful within a year and prices would decline. Manufacturing plans were abandoned and our purchase cost dropped 25% in the following fifteen months in the face of overwhelming supplies.

Price Forecasts:

I know how to make short-range price forecasts on volatile price materials as a basis for buying and inventory policy. While in charge of economic research for a previous employer, I made buying policy recommendations to three departments in purchases of oils and other industrial products which were in excess of fifty million dollars per year.

Manufacturing Costs:

I developed cost elements of products we purchased to assist buyers in setting objective price targets. For example, by building a cost estimate for a supplier from that of a similar product. I pointed out that a contract for a cyclic chemical was incorrectly weighed for raw material and labor inputs. The contract was revised with reduced costs of $65,000.

Value Analysis:

To improve results of value analysis projects, I organized and conducted meetings attended by personnel from division management, research, manufacturing and purchasing. This direct tapping of internal skills has paid off in purchasing cost reductions, has coordinated efforts on common problems and has stimulated on-the-spot discussions to improve purchasing service to divisions,

RESEARCH ON THE PURCHASING SYSTEM
Purchasing Policy and Reports:

I wrote a purchasing manual which was distributed to the twelve divisions of the company as a guide for purchasing operations. After six years, this booklet is still in use. I was assigned responsibility by the director of purchasing for writing monthly reports to company top management summarizing purchasing operations and developments.

Performance Evaluation:

After being asked to determine a better approach for measuring purchasing efficiency, I introduced a method involving both quantitative and qualitative objectives. I presented a paper on this subject at a recent meeting of the National Association of Purchasing Agents.

PROFESSIONAL AFFILIATIONS

Member, American Management Association and American Chemical Society

Contributor, professional journals

Chairman and speaker at American Marketing Association Seminars.

EDUCATIONAL AND PERSONAL DATA

Master of Science degree, Columbia University, 1960

Officer, church and civic organizations

Married, four school-age children

A CREATIVE ARTIST AND DESIGNER CROSSES OVER FROM FREE LANCE TO A FULL-TIME SALARIED POSITION WITH THIS RESUME

HERE is a good example of how it's possible to prove measurable results in even the most intangible kind of work. The nature of this applicant's work has forced her to use more quotes than our rule of "two or three to a résumé." But notice that she has been meticulous in selecting quotes which point directly to specific accomplishments in her work rather than just referring to general personal characteristics.

Another important feature of this résumé is the manner in which it is planned to overcome the employer's possible objections to hiring a free lance applicant for a full time job. Although this job hunter's experience has been 80 per cent free lance, she never uses the term "free lance." Rather, she sticks strictly and honestly to describing what she did, for whom and what resulted. Nowhere does she allow herself to wander into any defensive explanation of the fact that the work was free lance.

See also that the résumé starts right off in the first functional heading with mention of a full time job the applicant held once years ago. And it closes with another mention of that old job solely to suggest that she is not a "lone wolf" worker and can do well cooperating with others within a company framework on a nine to five basis. That is the sole reason for mentioning these jobs. Notice that the opening scope statement does not mention them. Rather it adheres strictly to that part of the applicant's background which applies to the job sought now in a commercial art studio.

Except for the expression "working under deadline pressure," this résumé does not describe the problems from one function to the next because the author reasoned that any statement of the problems would alter the picture of what she did and how she did it. It's true that in some instances a description of the problem will not add anything to your story. But if you consider not using problem identification in your résumé, be sure that you have good factual reason and are not just attempting the lazy way out. And remember, no matter what your level may be, never assume that because a prospective employer knows the business you are talking about, that he knows the particular problems you faced.

Elaine Sargent
165 East 48th Street
New York, New York 10017
212–755–7996

ARTIST – DESIGNER

I have ten years' creative planning and benchwork experience in commercial art and three-dimensional design mostly for national accounts in the food, home economy and fashion fields.

MAGAZINE LAYOUT & ART

I have planned the layout, worked up roughs and sometimes finished art and comprehensives for hundreds of magazine advertisements and product publicity features appearing in most of the leading women's service publications for accounts such as Burlington Mills, Coats & Clark, Pittsburgh Plate (Fiber Glass). On three occasions my layouts have been cited in features in *Advertising Age*. One recent publicity feature I worked out for another leading thread company was appraised by the general sales manager of the company in a letter saying, "We consider the Bulky Sweater promotion one of the finest stimulants to hand knitting that has come down the pike in a long time."

My earlier experience included four years as associate art editor for one of the large circulation women's service magazines. One of my editorial layouts for them won the Art Directors Club Medal (editorial art, fiction, two colors).

TELEVISION

I have designed and usually turned out hand-made product displays for television commercials which have appeared on the major networks. For example, for one of the aluminum foil manufacturers, I made an animal which I called "Dog-Gone-It" out of an aluminum pan and other of the client's products. Originally intended for a one-shot appearance, "Dog-Gone-It" was used a dozen times and later adapted for store display and a mail piece.

STORE DISPLAYS

I have designed and supervised production of store window displays used in 359 stores throughout the country. Characteristically, these displays have used advertised products and been constructed out of brand name fabrics, spools of thread, wall paper and candy, paper plates, doilies, straws, refrigerator dishes, contact tape, shelf paper and doilies.

Referring to one display of a brand name which I titled "Sparkle While You Work," one of the Philadelphia department stores wrote ". . . we had sellouts of the featured colors." And the manufacturer said ". . . our sales of this line more than tripled as compared to the same month the previous year."

COLLATERAL MERCHANDISING MATERIALS

I have created about thirty direct mail pieces in the last ten years, ranging from single fold black and white to more elaborate four-color pieces. Referring to the unique fold and color combination of one recent mail piece for a brand name fabric, the creative planning director of the advertising agency said, ". . . a really delightful, attention-getting device . . . terrific."

A crochet book I redesigned sold 66% more copies in eight months at a 75% higher price than the old book did in any one year for the previous seven years.

PRODUCTION

All of my print work has involved supervising production of art for rotogravure and letterpress following through from rough layout, supervising photography, specifying type, ordering mechanical lettering and retouching. I have assigned and worked with a hundred free lance artists on varied large and small pieces. I have worked with about twenty-five of the best-known photographers in the fashion and food fields and have discovered and helped develop ten previously little known photographers now regularly used by many of the 4 A agencies.

In my four years as a magazine associate art editor I coordinated monthly, working under deadline pressure, the work of eighteen editors, numerous free lance artists and fashion and home economy specialists. The director of production said I was the most efficient art editor in his twenty years on the staff.

EDUCATION

Rhode Island School of Design, graduated, 1952

ENERGETIC SMALL-BUSINESS SALES MANAGER
SELLS HIMSELF AT HIS BEST IN THIS
ATTENTION-GETTING RESUME

HERE is a good example of a résumé that clearly describes a man who lives and breathes his work and knows his job. It is another illustration of the effectiveness of showing interest and enthusiasm and a good sense of organization. Again, we remind you of the paramount importance of these elements in applying for a good job.

Interestingly enough, this applicant reached his new job in sales promotion rather than as sales manager as this résumé job title indicates. And the new job is one which deals in a somewhat different product from the one he emphasizes here. But, as is often the case, it was his drive and talent and resourcefulness as displayed in this résumé which led him to the job. Keep this in mind if you are afraid that a functional résumé slanted toward one type of job will limit your job market coverage.

Look for this applicant's illustrations of working with other people above him, below him and at his same level. If your job calls for any kind of association with fellow workers or customers and clients, make certain your résumé proves your capabilities in this area.

Walter Rowen
1082 Warburton Ave.
Yonkers, New York 10701
914–965–6173

SALES MANAGER

PLANNING SALES CAMPAIGNS

When I was made sales manager of a relatively small store fixture manufacturer, I was faced generally with the task of building new business, setting up a sales force and spreading our company name on a national scale.

After my own one-man survey of the market, I persuaded the company president and chief engineer to manufacture a standard line of fixtures for paint dealers because (1) this was a market related to hardware stores for whom we had a line of fixtures and we would be able to sell some of these fixtures to the paint industry and (2) the paint dealers at the time were far behind in store modernization and merchandizing and there wasn't any national fixture company offering a complete line of fixtures and a planning service.

Within three years after introducing this new line to the paint industry primarily by mailing catalogues to paint manufacturers and their sales representatives and by working closely with paint associations, our sales to the paint industry averaged over $500,000 per year.

HIRING AND TRAINING SALES PEOPLE

I hired and trained twenty sales people to cover the Midwest, New England and the Southeast. I worked with these individuals in their territories, teaching them store layout and how to present and sell our equipment. As an incentive to start them I turned over to them live prospects we had been working on before the sales people came to us. Then I kept in continuous close contact as they developed with us. Today, nine years later, eighteen of these twenty men and women are still with the company. Each of them is a producer, selling chains such as Montgomery Ward, Union Supply Co., Sunset Stores and A. C. Horn Company. Two of the original men have been established as regional sales managers and hired and trained their own sales personnel in the territory which I helped them develop.

SALES PROMOTION AND ADVERTISING LIAISON

To build our paint fixture line, I have organized and directed displays at trade conventions where I set up model stores complete with merchandise on display. Though the model stores took up about six times the space of the average booth, we paid only for a single booth, saving my company thousands of dollars. At one national convention, we wrote over $45,000 of fixture sales in three days, an increase of 60% more than the firm had ever done at a national convention prior to my association with them.

Lately, I worked with our engineers to develop a continuous tape recording machine that gives a predetermined sales message to a store customer when he steps on a mat or pushes a selecting button. We displayed this machine for the first time in our model store at a recent Chicago convention and it contributed importantly to bettering our previous convention sales record. In addition, manufacturers became interested in this machine to tie in with their point of purchase displays and we took orders to design and manufacture six of them. This adds a promising new profitable product to our line.

PUBLICITY AND ADVERTISING

Through contacts and friends I made, I was able to acquire sizable publicity coverage in about twenty various trade magazines showing some of our products and store installations. I wrote several articles on store modernization and merchandising display that appeared in publications such as *Paint Logic, American Paint and Wallpaper Dealer* and *Colorama.*

I have lectured on the same subjects at paint conventions and wallpaper conferences. At a recent conference I appeared on the same program with the chief of the Small Business Administration, and the director of marketing and business for the Board of Education, Washington, D.C. Most recently, I have lectured on power of visual merchandising at a sales training course conducted by the New York Paint Dealers Association.

I have continuously assisted our advertising man by suggesting types of fixtures to use in our magazine advertising and calling attention to publications I felt were worth investigating for our insertions. We have also worked together on much of our promotional material such as point-of-purchase materials and direct mail.

SELLING

In a previous job as salesman for another store fixture manufacturer, I developed an unproductive market in the New York area to over $100,000 per year to independent dealers. This was done without benefit of any consequential advertising.

The first year we introduced our paint fixtures, I marketed them in a variety of other areas to discover customer needs and objections prior to committing us to final production designs.

PRODUCT KNOWLEDGE

I received my early training in carpentry and drafting at vocational schools and was employed for three years by a contractor who specialized in remodeling store fronts, display counters and shelves and lighting.

PERSONAL

Age 35, married, two children
Secretary, New York Paint Dealers' Association

WITH PERSONAL CONTACTS EXHAUSTED AFTER
SEVEN MONTHS OF PROBING OLD ACQUAINTANCES,
A MID-CAREER PLANT MANAGER ESTABLISHES
ENTIRELY NEW CONTACTS WITH THIS RESUME
AND GETS THE JOB HE WANTS

WHEN Clifford Reagan was forced to resign out of personal differences with his employer, he traveled from pillar to post "asking around" among his many long time business friends. As is often the case, this sort of hit and miss job hunting yielded only a few polite interviews and one near miss.

It took this forceful functional résumé to turn the tide with facts and figures which leave no question about this applicant's ability. Look at the results in this résumé. They carry much more weight than any friendly luncheon date or casual phone call for help.

Read between the lines too. Without expressing any naive personal opinion about himself, this applicant clearly indicates his ability to get along well with people above him, below him and at his same level.

Most importantly, he shows his hand at work as a tactful customer relations man with a watchful eye on holding established clients and creating profitable new business. These qualifications are key features which distinguish this plant manager from the run-of-the-mill.

When you complete the first draft of your résumé, don't forget to check every paragraph you have written with the question, "Does this distinguish me from the average?"

Clifford R. Regan
Tufts Avenue
Royal Oak, Michigan 48067
517–466–2189

PLANT MANAGER

PLANNING

It's the year 1954. Auto-Label Machinery Division of American-Standard Corp. had developed a rotary air oven for baking metal decorated sheets for the canning industry. They were manufacturing and selling this oven, two a month at $40,000 each. At this time I joined the company and through planning with management and working with engineering and purchasing, we developed various types of improved ovens. By 1967, a direct external oven was being manufactured at the rate of four per month at a selling price of $160,000 each, an increase in business of 800% in thirteen years.

In 1970, one of Auto-Label's biggest customers, West Coast Packing Corp., bought out a smaller packing company in Sarnia, Canada. The new acquisition included a separate machinery division at Dundee.

West Coast wanted some equipment manufactured conveniently nearby and put the job up for bid to several Canadian plants including their subsidiary at Dundee. When the bids were returned, we were consulted for advice. All of them seemed high, including one for $178,000 from their own Dundee plant where they preferred to have the work done.

As a goodwill gesture for my employer, I traveled to Dundee and worked with the managing director, plant superintendent and purchasing department to help them revamp their plans. We reduced their estimate approximately 200%. This was also about 70% of the amount of other bidding Canadian plants, so Dundee got the order. I went to Dundee for one week to help them set up work procedures and again later on for another week to assist in increasing production efficiency when they were running the job. As a result, they were able to achieve a 20% savings in labor costs for a first time run of this type of work in their plant.

When the work was completed, West Coast Packing wrote and telephoned us, "You have saved us considerable cost . . . and helped us over a difficult hump . . . We will not soon forget it."

"You have saved us considerable cost ... and helped us over a difficult hump ... We will not soon forget it."

PRODUCTION

At Auto-Label, one of our many problems was handling sheet metal duct work in mass production. Working with engineering and design departments, we reduced bending and forming operations for a savings of over 50%. The volume of this work amounted to an average of $400,000 per year.

In another position as production control supervisor for Mid-Continent Container Division of Mid-Continent Steel Corp., I revised printing production procedures on metal and box oven operations to reduce material and labor costs 8% per unit representing an annual saving of about $72,000 without any sacrifice in quality production.

SUB-CONTRACTING AND ESTIMATING

In 1943 I instituted the subcontracting system which is still in effect at Auto-Label. Subcontracting of iron frame work and piping orders now amounts to about $3,500,000 annually.

On one special project to manufacture equipment in Canada for the newest Mid-Continent Container Division plant there, I subcontracted all the work to gain a savings of approximately 30%, $58,000 under United States costs.

At a time when materials were available in limited allotments, Auto-Label was forced into diversified activity to keep operating. After their six months of estimating and receiving work against these estimates without profit, I was assigned to review the conditions. Investigation revealed that our estimators were not familiar with this diversified type of work so I took over this phase of our activity. During the next three years of estimating on about $40,000,000 of business, we received over $9,000,000 of profitable business.

DESIGN AND DEVELOPMENT

In coordination with a sales engineer at Auto-Label, a 150-sheet-per-minute, 4-zone, direct external fired coating oven was designed and manufactured. This oven is now used as the standard type by most of the nation's leading can manufacturers.

Working in conjunction with three other engineers, the first all direct external fired oven for baking and coating on flat sheets for steel containers was developed. This is the industry-wide-publicized oven, first of its kind to be used by Remco Manufacturing, Inc.

Now a quantity of decorated sheets sufficient to manufacture a freight car full of steel barrels can be stocked in space taking up no more room than a small row boat.

As oven designer in charge for Mid-Continent, I redesigned six ovens, iron work structurals, duct work, panels and automatic sheet handling machinery to achieve a 30% to 36% reduction in manufacturing costs.

PURCHASING

For ten years under my supervision, the purchasing department at Auto-Label executed orders for approximately $6,000,000 per year of inventory and special services equipment.

INDUSTRIAL RELATIONS

I worked with our administrative team to establish formalized personnel practices. Copies of this were published and distributed to employees to create the proper understanding between management and labor. The first year of this practice, personnel turnover reduced from 8% to 3% and has held at that level or below for five years since.

EDUCATION

M. E. Degree, Rensselaer Polytechnic Institute, 1952

PERSONAL

Married, three children. Member A.S.M.E. & N.A.P.A.